**THE CALL
IS COMING
FROM INSIDE
THE HOUSE**

ALLYSON McOUAT

THE CALL IS COMING FROM INSIDE THE HOUSE

ESSAYS

This book is also available as a Global Certified Accessible™ (GCA) ebook. ECW Press's ebooks are screen reader friendly and are built to meet the needs of those who are unable to read standard print due to blindness, low vision, dyslexia, or a physical disability.

Purchase the print edition and receive the ebook free. For details, go to ecwpress.com/ebook.

Published by ECW Press
665 Gerrard Street East
Toronto, Ontario, Canada M4M 1Y2
416-694-3348 / info@ecwpress.com

Editor for the Press: Pia Singhal
Copy editor: Rachel Ironstone
Cover design: Jessica Albert and Caroline Suzuki
Cover image: Sarah Detweiler / Paradigm Gallery + Studio

To the best of her abilities, the author has related experiences, places, people, and organizations from her memories of them. In order to protect the privacy of others, she has, in some instances, changed the names of certain people and details of events and places.

LIBRARY AND ARCHIVES CANADA CATALOGUING IN PUBLICATION

Title: The call is coming from inside the house : essays / Allyson McOuat.

Names: McOuat, Allyson, author.

Identifiers: Canadiana (print) 20230561837 | Canadiana (ebook) 20230561853

ISBN 978-1-77041-755-7 (softcover)
ISBN 978-1-77852-282-6 (ePub)
ISBN 978-1-77852-283-3 (PDF)

Subjects: LCGFT: Essays.

Classification: LCC PS8625.O93 C35 2024 | DDC C814/.6—dc23

This book is funded in part by the Government of Canada. *Ce livre est financé en partie par le gouvernement du Canada.* We acknowledge the support of the Canada Council for the Arts. *Nous remercions le Conseil des arts du Canada de son soutien.* We acknowledge the funding support of the Ontario Arts Council (OAC), an agency of the Government of Ontario. We also acknowledge the support of the Government of Ontario through the Ontario Book Publishing Tax Credit, and through Ontario Creates.

PRINTED AND BOUND IN CANADA

PRINTING: MARQUIS 5 4 3 2 1

MIX
Paper from responsible sources
FSC www.fsc.org FSC® C103567

In memory of my mother, Lila Anne Holland,
who would want me to tell you that I can also sing
and dance. And for my daughters, Tatum and Georgia,
who make me want to sing and dance.

Vanity Fair: What do you regard as the
lowest depth of misery?
David Bowie: Living in fear.

I'm not interested in everyday reality, but in the
reality of the heart. I like fantasy, like a fairy tale.
I'm interested in shadows and contrasts.

— GENE WILDER

CONTENTS

THE PLAYLIST

Prologue: Into The Woods
Goodbye Horses, Q Lazzarus
A Forest, The Cure

The Harbinger
Escape Myself, Nouvelle Vague
Looking for Clues, Robert Palmer

The Haunted House
The House That We Built, Alisha's Attic

The Haunted
You're the One That I Want, Lo-Fang

The Storyteller
Stand by Me, Tracy Chapman

The Teenage Girls
Freedom! '90, George Michael

The Pregnant Woman
Three Babies, Sinéad O'Connor

The Fortune Teller
Cross Bones Style, Cat Powers

The Crone, The Maiden, and the Raccoon
Regret, New Order
Female of the Species, Space

The Bitch
Bridges, Destiny's Child

The Man at the End of the Bed
Bad Dream, Cannons

The Babysitter
This City Never Sleeps, Eurythmics
Boys Wanna Be Her, Peaches

The Psycho Chick
Human Behaviour, Björk

The Victim
I Will Survive, Cake
Rising, Lhasa de Sela

The Coven

Magic, Olivia Newton John

Epilogue: Love is Digging The Grave

Without You, Without Them, boygenius

Bonus:

Video Vérité, Blue Peter

PROLOGUE

INTO THE WOODS WE GO

"Into the woods and through the fear,
you have to take the journey."

— STEPHEN SONDHEIM

A spring ambles across the back of my parents' property, right between their home and the adjacent twenty-seven-acre forest. I haven't lived here for over two decades, choosing instead to raise my family in Toronto. For a long time I considered myself an urban person rather than a suburban one — falling for another useless form of binary determinism that you must always be one thing or another. But now that I am nearing the end of my forties, I see I exist on the sub/urban spectrum. It is true that even a distance as relatively small as forty kilometres can seem like a different world, but I love this creek, this house, this neighbourhood. The time of my life spent growing up in the suburbs, especially from 1980 to 2000, shaped me into the queer woman I am today, and the city gave me a safe place to live that life. I grew up with many privileges in a two-parent home that was one of thousands of contemporary two-parent, cookie-cutter households like it. Our home held delightful secrets in the backyard, a path through wild gardens with wonderland-like flowers the size of dinner plates that led to a grass covered hill, down to the stream, all enclosed in a shaded glen with the towering trees of a forest all around. Sheltered twice over, as the suburbs in general were heavily protected from any perceived negative influences from alternative culture. We had a wide selection of mainstream films shown at our local theatre and available for rent at the corner Blockbuster. The local HMV carried chart-topping records and songs from the British Invasion of the 1990s but not much else. I was discouraged from watching anything in the horror genre because it wasn't ladylike. Like most families in the suburbs in the '80s, ours followed the trends — little girls took skating and dance classes and little boys played hockey and soccer. Little boys could watch *Friday the 13th* and little girls could watch *Anne of Green Gables*; it kept things simple. But I was drawn to complexities. So, whenever I would come across something subversive or outstandingly baroque, like *Orlando*, the amorphous Tilda Swinton–starring film adaptation of Virginia Woolf's work, I would yearn for more.

Despite its limitations, the spot I grew up in now feels like a magical, restorative land to me, and I am not alone in that assessment. For ten thousand years, Indigenous groups like the Huron-Wendat, Haudenosaunee, and Anishinaabe called this area home before the original British Invasion. In 1805, the land was included in the Toronto Purchase as Treaty 13, and by the late 1800s, Spring Creek, as it was called, was considered something of a fountain of youth — drinking from it was said to give long life. A local hotel, long since shuttered, once described the creek in their advertising as "embowed in a sylvan grove . . . its spring water is far famed for its miraculous cures." The stream became an attraction that made our small town a destination for health-conscious tourists. I never tire of exploring this forest and stream because, as it is with life, your view changes dramatically with every season. In the winter, the forest is gray and quiet, and some mornings you can spy the seven local deer walking through the brush. In the summer, the woods are verdant and noisy with the call of birds and chatter of squirrels. The spring is sometimes frightening because the riverbanks often flood and threaten to rise up to the back door.

My father calls it the Storybook House because everything in the antique-filled house, from the brass doorknobs to the cutlery, holds a story. And I guess, now, this book about the subversive, dangerous, and supernatural stories that shaped me will be part of the Storybook House too. Every day there is another story to tell. Although as a mother and cis-femme, queer woman, I've struggled with centring my stories and experiences, separating the expectations of my role from my individual being, and, as they say in *Orlando*, not drowning "anonymously in the milk of female kindness." We must stay sweet, calm, and sheltered.

On a recent autumn evening, an ex-lover and I were visiting with my parents and decided to walk my two-year-old English bulldog pandemic puppy. We strolled down the main road from home hand-in-hand and stopped in a suburban playground that was on the edge of our forest to take in the bright stars and the full moon. It was exactly the kind of late autumn atmosphere that makes for either a romance movie or a horror film — a gentle breeze blowing a smattering of leaves off the trees, a crisp temperature, a layer of fog-like mist in the air — although, romance and horror are sometimes linked for me. I always feel scared when I think about trying to fall in love again with some new person, a stranger. The time it takes to get to know someone intimately. The risks. I've had some heartbreaks that were so painful they took years to recover from. She was one of them. We paused on the edge of the unlit soccer field to look up at the night sky and explore the constellations via a handy app on her phone.

We were delighted at how the app instantaneously displayed both the bright stars we could clearly see right in front of us, with the added bonus of including those stars that were too far in the distance to discern or were covered by clouds. An animated line on her screen bounced from one invisible star millions of miles away from us to another, connecting them all into a picture of a bear. Eons of myth, complicated scientific measurements, distant satellites, detailed coding, stories told around ancient campfires, and cutting-edge communications technology collided in this one godlike app that we tiny mortals could now access with the touch of a finger. It was amazing, but at the same time I was experiencing an uncomfortable sensation of vulnerability. Not dissimilar to something called thalassophobia, a reverse kind of claustrophobia that I'd experienced only once before while snorkeling in the ocean; a realization that the water has no walls or doors. It was wide open all around me for miles, and I was sharing this incomprehensibly enormous space with billions of sea creatures. Sharks, giant blue whales, eels and barracuda, clown fish and octopi. I was completely exposed and as tiny and irrelevant to this whole ecosystem as the shell on one single hermit crab out of the tens of millions in the ocean —

easily discarded when my usefulness to the environment was complete.

"Oh! And also," she chimed, shaking her short white curls in excitement as she looked down at the grass and dirt below us, "I can show you the stars on the other side of the world right now, as if we were looking right through the centre of the Earth and coming out the other side."

"Great!" I said.

As she turned her screen down towards the ground, my dog, silent but agitated, strained against her red leather collar in the direction of the forest. She seemed desperate to explore, her wrinkled nose furiously sniffing the air. As she lunged, her leash tangled around the legs of my friend, pulling me into her leather jacket. Our legs wound together just like the beginning of *101 Dalmatians*, my gray high-heeled boots against her jeans. We rolled our eyes and scoffed at the Hallmarkian accuracy of the dog's timing as we untangled each other from our constraints. It has been obvious to everyone around us that something still existed in the space between her and me. They wanted answers as to why we weren't together anymore. The truth was that we simply weren't compatible in ways we consider too private to discuss publicly, so instead we don't talk about it at all.

As I bent down to unleash the dog, I paused and followed my pup's gaze. That's when I saw movement in the dark. It explained why she was so agitated. She knew something was there. A spectral form slowly moving alongside us. Mesmerized as the shape emerged out of the shadows, I tried to adjust my eyes to see what I was looking at. A small deer? No. Definitely a dog. But black as pitch; it was positively ghostly. I even thought for a millisecond that I could see right through the animal to the trees behind. The closer it came, the clearer it became. It was a wolflike creature. Its back and head were planked, its ears laid down tight to its head. It was stalking us.

My friend quietly told me to walk slowly out of the park, backwards, and as we did, she gallantly stepped between me and the beast. My dog bounded excitedly along beside me. I felt ridiculous, but I did as she instructed and slowly and steadily tiptoed my way backwards up the path and out of the park, while trying to keep an eye on the animal. The coyote slipped back into complete concealment and disappeared, leaving no trace.

Despite growing up right next to these woods, I realized then that I actually knew very little of its spirit. This whole time I had been childishly romanticizing the trees, when all the while I had been looking out over a forest full of impossibly beautiful dangers.

Comforted by the bright streetlamps of the main roadway, we paused for a deep breath before continuing on, nervously laughing about how close we had come to danger without knowing. As we walked down the road back towards my parents' home, we talked about other people who had been in similar situations and how they'd handled it. We recalled articles and advice we had read about facing down wildlife, TikToks and YouTube videos. Should it come back again, my friend suggested that we run for the nearest house and knock on the door. I said I wouldn't disturb one of my neighbours this late unless pursued by Michael Myers and he was on an electric scooter.

I haphazardly darted a quick look backwards just to make sure the coyote hadn't followed us out onto the street. And sure enough — there he was. Only twenty feet behind us, having left the safety of the forest and loping brazenly down the middle of the roadway in full evening street light. Now that I could really see him, I confirmed that the animal was larger than any coyote I had ever seen. He was huge and black and fluffy, like a wolf. My, what big ears he had, long and now perked up, listening intently. And my, what big eyes he had, black and steady and locked on us. And my, what long legs he had ... as he switched from a trot into a full-blown sprint towards us.

We shrieked with fear and took off running, she in sensible sneakers and I in my trademarked inappropriate footwear, the dog looking at me as if to say, "*Now* you run? I told you to run ten minutes ago!" We all ran together down the entire length of the street towards my parents' house and, honestly, the wolf must not have been putting his all behind it because we beat him to the door, and we are not sprinters. Of course, I scrambled at the door to find my keys, dropping them and picking them back up again in another cliché of a horror film. On seeing that we were as good as inside, the animal stopped his pursuit and loped away down another street instead.

Afterwards, laughing and breathlessly recounting this story to family inside and via group FaceTimes, we were first dismissed: *A wolf? In the suburbs? You lie!* But once they believed us, the interrogation began. *How big was it really? I thought you said you couldn't see it? Are you sure it wasn't a German Shepherd? Did it really chase you, or was it just running in the same direction? Do you really think it was trying to kill you?* And then finally, the blaming: *Well, what were you doing walking your dog at night? And near a forest? Oh my God, I would never do that! Look, you really need to be more careful.*

I didn't know how to answer their skepticism and judgment. Yes, there was a large, wolflike animal that was following us, and yes it ran down the street towards us. But I don't know what was going on in the creature's mind, I didn't stop to psycho-analyze it like a bespeckled Road Runner plunking Wile E. Coyote down on a couch and pulling out a notepad. I do not know if the animal planned to grab my chubby little dog by the scruff and take off with her, or if he was going to attack one of us, or if he was simply out stretching his legs a bit on a cool fall evening and enjoyed making middle-aged women squeal and run away like chickens.

What good did questioning our story do? I felt I had done my due diligence: I informed them all of the threat in the neighbourhood, *There is a beast in the forest!* I've accomplished that in an easily digestible way, by entertaining them with self-deprecating jokes about my inappropriate footwear. I've hopefully made them think twice about forest safety after dark. I've even brought along a witness to corroborate who is known to be beyond reproach. And they still don't believe me. But their believing me doesn't change the fact that it happened. And I will never be able to make *everything* clear for them. We ask the impossible of our non-fiction writers.

I suppose you must understand before heading any further into this book that, like this story, not every story will be complete or simple or contain one hundred percent God's honest truth, for myriad reasons which I will further illuminate throughout. Instead, in the retelling of stories, I will — as we all do — hopscotch from one chalk-drawn, logic-filled square to another, all towards the tossed pebble at the finish, but likely skipping numbers along the way, missing the larger leaps I am not bold enough to take, approaching only the faintest outline of an answer, the bulk of which has blown away in the wind.

As a Gen Xer who witnessed the rise of home video, cable television, personal computers, and the early stages of the internet, my generation had unprecedented access to movies, music, and literature. It was how we explored different perspectives, challenged conventions, and shaped our own identities. So, any story I tell is also inevitably shaped by the media of my time, the stories that resonated with me that often captured the rebellious and independent spirit of my generation, addressed themes of alienation, individualism, and skepticism toward authority.

And, as I am preparing for this journey solo, any recounting will unfortunately be devoid of the entirety afforded by the varying perspectives of all people involved. Because surely there were conversations I was not privy to. Feelings that others were too scared or shy to share. History, prejudices, and belief systems that I could never access; books I haven't read, speeches I haven't heard. My mind alone is available to frame this narrative, using the information and recollections I have gleaned from my own place of privilege, prejudice, and personal experience. And also, my mind is prone to meandering. In other words, this series of stories will be exactly like every other story ever told in the history of humankind — a partial snapshot of a much larger and expansive, infinite landscape, most of which is not visible. That may be unsettling, thalassophobic even, to those who want binary logic and irrefutable clarity.

We have to access vulnerability both when we look at our truth and when we listen to someone else's, because it requires trust. That's why the tension that true stories create is a very frightening thing for many people — because trust is vulnerability, and vulnerability is frightening. Because we all have been told that only terror lies in wait in the places where the invisible reigns, and that's where we have to go to find the truth.

How I wish I could tour you around the entirety of my stories and highlight important historical aspects. I dream about saying with concrete confidence that "this exact thing happened right here," and "this did not." I wish I could be like my friend's constellation app and save you the frustration of looking for meaning in the chaos and instead highlight all the stars with a laser pointer. Because the one thing I know definitively is that the greatest torments I have experienced in my several decades of life grew from the places where the complete picture was denied me.

We know how important truth is. Rule number one of *The Boy* (or, in my case, woman) *Who Cried Wolf* is "tell the truth, or the townspeople will let you get ripped apart by wolves." Without some tactile, tangible, concept of truth that we can ground ourselves to, we risk being left floating about with unsettled spirits.

I suppose that's why as clever pattern makers, when we humans miss the lines between stars, we will draw our own. When we don't have the complete story, we will automatically stretch logic in directions it wasn't meant to go and then fall for fallacies instead of exerting the patience we need to wait for confirmation. We form our own conclusions.

It's not our fault we are wired this way, particularly women of Generation X. The first to head home after school to the empty house of working parents. Parents with more complex personal lives than ever before, with divorce and remarriage rates higher than ever. We were raised on TV, movies, and stories that modified society's new complex, uncomfortable truths and mixed them up with an amalgamation of ancient and urban myths, generalized threats, and sometimes even a little sprinkle of gore on top to scare children straight. We started out young, being soothed to sleep with fairy tales about half-dead princesses and the witches and hags who cursed them, folk tales about giant trolls hiding under bridges — and then wonder why as adults we all get so anxious at bedtime. Through these stories, we learned how vulnerable we are when our truth gets into the hands of the unscrupulous. Once the wolf knows where you are going, he will run faster than you, right for the cottage, and take whatever is most valuable to you, like your sweet Nana. These stories taught us to constantly question what truths are told to us. Because a nightgown on a wolf doesn't make her your Nana even if she tells you she is. (It's still identity theft and probably transphobic.) These stories ingrained in us the idea that on our path through life, we will inevitably come close to danger because it's always around us, waiting for the right time to attack. Sometimes it's even right there in your own family.

It's no wonder that as we age, we are drawn to adult versions of these same cautionary tales in the form of bloody horror films about unrelenting monsters chasing down women, true-crime podcasts about real-life missing women and children, and limited series about grizzled detectives close to retirement wanting to wrap up this one last case. These tales serve a purpose beyond teaching us roundabout lessons and morals. They give us a legitimate, concrete focal point for our overwhelming, existential anxieties about what terrors may await us. They answer our questions and give us a clarity we can sink our teeth into. The murkiness of nuance and endless possibilities will always be scarier than the grisliest of solid truths.

And then there are the other reasons people are afraid of what's hidden in the nuance.

For those of us who identify as queer in my generation, we know that there is a phantasmic mix of fear and excitement in what information we choose to hold back — two emotions which manifest in the exact same physical symptoms: butterflies appearing out of nowhere and rustling about inside your stomach, the hairs on your arms and the back of your neck elevating, breath held. For those of us with fluid queer identities that may for years be lesbian, and then for a time be bi or pan, we know what it is to be considered the invisible monster, whispered about as a person without a strong identity, the traitor to the community, a double agent who slips in and out of the culture, letting ourselves be seen and unseen when it's convenient for us.

Society has conditioned us to be hypervigilant against anyone who seems to be hiding part of their nature in plain sight. Our true-crime-obsessed media is predominantly dedicated to feeding into this fear by trying to deconstruct the psychology behind the killers who walked amongst us hiding their violent, psychopathic tendencies: Ted Bundy, John Wayne Gacy, Paul Bernardo and Karla Homolka, Bruce McArthur, and others. A heartless killer could be standing right there in front of you in their very own skin and be someone completely different from the person you have been utterly convinced they were the whole time.

Homophobia fed on this. Others recognized someone with a secret and saw it as dangerous; but it wasn't violence queer people were hiding — it was love. Once someone's true self is uncovered, that truth can be life-altering, terrifying, and dangerous, or it might be brilliantly, blindingly, wonderfully revealing and celebratory. Either way, we are all better for knowing the truth about each other.

Wading through the fog of nuance to reach the clarity of truth might be frightening, but I think I'm still going to go looking for it. Because believing in ourselves, living our own stories, trusting our own experiences and influences, understanding how they shaped us, that is how we develop the unextinguishable light within us, the fire that keeps us warm at night. No one benefits when you let others tell you what to think or how to feel about your own experiences, or what you should enjoy.

With my coyote, should I have questioned whether to feel frightened? What if I had taken the time to stop and consider what people would think about my reaction, instead of running? Would my pudgy little dog be coyote feed now? Everyone's experience of what they see as a threat and what sparks their own fear is unique to their journey. The only way to really understand another person is to walk the same pathway and witness the monsters they faced deep in the woods.

THE HARBINGER

(DEATH AT EVERY CORNER)

Outside gets inside through her skin. I've been
out before but this time it's much safer in.

— KATE BUSH, *Breathing*

Look, I knew it was coming. It was an inevitable torture. All I could do was brace myself for the words as they left her tiny little mouth and the sounds entered the atmosphere. "Mommy? We watch Fwozen?" This would be our 9,756th viewing of the cartoon this week. Her eyes were enormous bright blue magnets searching deep into my soul and attracting my bottomless generosity for her. *Frozen* is a movie about a young queen embracing her icy inner superpower after her frightened parents are warned by a mystical rock troll that their daughter's magic is powerful and fear would be her enemy. They take the rock troll's words to mean that other people's fear is their daughter's enemy, and they train her to be afraid of *herself* instead, forcing her to mask for her entire childhood.

Many people speculate about Elsa's sexuality. One of the first female Disney characters without an obvious love interest,

Elsa has been queer-coded as lesbian, bi, aromantic, or asexual. I like the film. The message is one I want my children to know, that when you embrace what makes you different instead of being scared of it, your outfits and hairstyle will improve, as will your overall outlook on life. Don't shut out love when it's offered. Set boundaries, build your own castle, but keep the door open. So, I said, "Yes, sweetheart," and shuffled her and her little sister into the living room and up on the couch to start the sisterly bonding early.

Queer-coding in film is something that started in the 1930s when the Hays morality code was established. Queerness became built into subtext through exaggerated mannerisms, tone of voice or lisps, bold fashion choices, or occupations. For generations, the more overtly queer the character, the stronger the ultimate punishment for their "sins." It's one of the reasons most of the queer-coded characters in Disney films are villains, like Scar, Ursula, and Captain Hook.

Elsa is queer-coded almost immediately by Grand Pabbie, the troll who acts as the Harbinger in *Frozen*, the mystical rock troll that the girls' parents take them to after Anna has been accidentally zapped in the head with Elsa's magic. Her ability to bend the natural order at her wish is subtext for stepping outside heteronormativity. When the troll asks Elsa's parents if she was "born with the powers or cursed," he may as well be asking if queerness is nature or nurture. When he warns Elsa that there is great danger in her power, he is essentially saying that she will face ignorance and bigotry in her lifetime if she uses her powers publicly. And he encourages her to control her power — meaning, know when it's safe to show your true self and when you have to mask it for your own safety. But he also gives her some positive messaging, illuminating that there will be great beauty in her power, which there always is when it comes to love.

I started to fade out a bit as we listened to the calming strains: *Na na na heyana, hahiyaha naha, Naheya heya na yanuwa, Anhahe yunuwana.* Apparently (according to Google), the opening song was based on a Sami yoik. A yoik is a unique cultural expression similar to singing, but really, it's more than that. A yoik is more like a spell, designed to conjure up those who have been lost and form a living image of them in sound. A yoik neither begins nor ends, it just *is*. Some yoiks have words, some don't. Some are rhythms or hand gestures. But this one has lyrics, and they are loosely translated to: "Times must come. Times must roll. Family must follow the family's path."

I was cradling my two-year-old on my lap when an image of her falling flashed in front of my eyes. I could almost hear the sound her skull made as it *thunk*ed against the floor. I winced and rubbed her pyjama-clad back, warm and soft, knowing she was safe here, draped across my body. But the image was powerful, like it was all happening again right that second and not as it had actually happened — a long time before when she was only three and a half months old.

She was lying in the middle of our king-size bed, surrounded by a barricade of folded laundry and kicking her chubby little feet in the air to grab at them. I remember she captured a pink toe, perfectly sized to fit inside her lips, and I felt a little jealous of her flexibility. I wandered back and forth between her and the dresser, slipping some shirts into the second drawer. The afternoon was sunny and bright, and reminiscent of the greatest mid-afternoon nap I had ever stolen, curled up in a sunbeam with my eldest daughter when she was a newborn like two contented kitties. I turned back towards the bed just in time to witness a momentous milestone. One I hadn't been expecting her to reach until she was another month or two older. Her first roll. Or rather, in her case, rolls. My baby had turned herself all the way over, and instead of stopping there, she must have turned a second time, bypassing the laundry, because she was teetering on the edge of the bed three feet from the floor.

My fight/flight/freeze/fawn response is always freeze. So, it seemed for a moment that we were both suspended in time before launching into the air. Her falling towards the hardwood and me leaping towards her, arms outstretched. My body failed us. My fingers were too short, my form too heavy, my muscles still weak from the C-section and bedrest. I missed catching her by a quarter of an inch. We were both silent from shock before her eyes welled with tears and the ear-splitting shrieking began. I raced her to the hospital, and thankfully she was absolutely fine, there was no skull fracture, no concussion, no damage at all. Not even a bruise. It was an accident, I had to constantly remind myself. There was no reason to think she might fall. But every now and then my body stiffens, and my mind becomes stuck in that moment. I will never put my babies in potential danger because I can see it all around me now; every possible scenario that could cause pain I have analyzed the second we walk in the room. My now ex-wife used to call my superpower Death at Every Corner. I like to playfully personify it now as my own personal Harbinger of Doom.

The Harbinger is the character at the beginning of every horror story that warns the characters of what is about to befall them. The ominous gas station attendant; the odd-ball townie like "Crazy" Ralph in *Friday the 13th*, who warns the teenagers to stay away from Camp Blood; the terrified local in a Stephen King short story who runs into the grocery store screaming, "There's something in the mist!" If you are looking for them, you'll usually find the Harbinger somewhere around a run-down old gas station, because their sole purpose is to add fuel to the plot line. Gas us all up so we can get to the scary part a little faster. The Harbinger is glaringly obvious and demands our attention, leaping out of dark corners, cutting the characters off at the pass, sometimes even following them all the way to the scene of the future crime to warn them again. You can't ignore the Harbinger, and yet the lead characters *always* do. If Michelle Mancini of 1998's *Urban Legend* had patiently waited for Michael McDonnell's stutter to play out so he could finish his sentence (instead of macing him and subsequently nearly running him over with her SUV), she would have heard him yell that there was "someone in the back seat" and saved herself an axe to the face two minutes later. The Harbinger knows the geography; this is their territory. They have been here before, and yet still the main characters brush them off as hysterics. And I understand why: The Harbinger is scary! Loud, jarring, comes at you by surprise, is terribly inconvenient to your plans, and sometimes a little drunk.

Almost immediately after my ex and I separated, my inner Harbinger started working overtime. I think at first it was a somewhat reasonable by-product of being the only adult in the house now, responsible for two tiny girls and a blind dog. I was exhausted down to the marrow of my bones, both sleep-deprived and totally grief-stricken from what seemed to be the sudden loss of my marriage. Add to that a sprinkling of fear from living in a potentially haunted house that came with its own brand of creepy surprises to navigate day and night, and within a few months, my Harbinger was becoming unbearable, demanding my attention with the intensity of an overtired toddler.

That night, I lifted my child off me and walked into the kitchen. The children always had to be in the same room as me, even though the house was open concept. So, my little shadows followed behind me, practically attached to my feet. One stopped at the pint-sized craft table that their mama had made to fit all baby things neatly and stylishly into the corner, and she picked up some safety scissors to casually clip out one thousand pieces of scrap paper and scatter them across the floor, one of her favourite pastimes. The sound of the scissors rhythmically snip, snip, snipping was both several feet away from me and right inside my ear at the same time. *Snip. Snip. Snip. Snip. Snipsnipsnipsnipsnip.* I tried not to anticipate the sound, the pause, the second of silence when the scissors stopped cutting because the blades had found the flesh of her thumb instead. But it didn't happen that time. She continued to happily distribute little confetti-sized pieces of pink construction paper all over the floor while I began preparing the evening bottle for my littlest, who had toddled over and tugged on my pant leg.

"Uppa! Uppa!" she cried. "No, sweetie, Mommy's doing something," I said, as the clicking of the knob released a stream of gas and a blue flame appeared on the stove. My inner Harbinger jumped out at me to say, "Look out! Fire!" because gas stoves always make me recall the story I was told about the time my brother and his friends almost died at a backyard barbeque.

Our family friend once threw a dinner party with his then-husband to celebrate redecorating their kitchen. It had been a massive renovation, and their home was absolutely stunning. I have heard some people speculate that our friend had "ti many martoonis" (as he would say) and had left the lid down when he lit the grill, letting all of the gas build up under the lid. Others said it was probably a leak in the propane tank. Whatever the reason, when he went to put the shish kebabs on, he touched the barbeque lighter to the pilot and, according to the witnesses, a massive ball of fire appeared in the air above the grill. Flames blazed out from underneath the barbeque. My friend screamed *Dive!* and his table full of fabulous guests hurled themselves over the railing of the deck and onto the grass below to avoid the explosion. The new kitchen was completely destroyed, but no one was badly hurt, thank God. And we were safe here today, I told my Harbinger. I took a deep breath and continued stirring, warming the milk up, with my shadow at my feet. Both kids blissfully unaware of the simmering stress happening underneath my calm exterior. "Go, sweetie, go away from the hot stove," I shooed her away to play. I worry that no matter what I do, I am destined to infuse them with my anxiety.

This evening, like every evening, continued on in the same way, with both of my children and the Harbinger competing for my attention. By bedtime, my body would inevitably cave to the stress, and I would fall asleep with the girls at 8:30 or 9 p.m., all piled into the same big bed. I initiated a family bed for the three of us immediately upon becoming a single parent, for safety, comfort, and convenience, as my toddler would wake almost hourly from the day she came home from the hospital until after her fifth birthday.

In dreams, like Freddy Krueger, my Harbinger would continue showing me potential stressors; a memory of some other person's trauma that would bubble up from my subconscious and become my own. The Harbinger hollering at me — "You'll get them all killed if you don't listen to me!" — I would wake with hard balls of knots under the thin skin of my shoulder blades.

But he hasn't always been there.

My omnipresent Harbinger seemed to arrive out of nowhere one day in a big bang and went on to build innumerable worlds of trouble for me. My first memory of him appearing goes back to when I was sticking my behind with needles every night and starting every morning off with an internal ultrasound wand, a phallic joystick wielded by a stranger, trying for a baby. My then-wife and I had gone to see the movie called *Across the Universe*, when I suddenly became extremely dizzy, short of breath, and felt faint and afraid. I sat on a bench and clutched at my ex's arm while she tried to calm me down. The movie hadn't been an upsetting one. We were not fighting. There was no trigger other than the theatre itself.

A year before, in 2006, I had started miscarrying our twins at almost twelve weeks while watching a mediocre Canadian buddy comedy film called *Bon Cop, Bad Cop* in that same theatre. My mother-in-law, a retired nurse, had come looking for me in the theatre's accessible bathroom where I had gone to find privacy and was crying while trying to clean myself up. She assessed me, took off her beige trench coat, wrapped it around my waist, and put her hand under my chin with her trademark loving strength. "Don't break down here. Don't you dare break down here. We are going to walk out of this bathroom and across the floor with our heads up high." She wrapped her arm around my shoulders tightly enough to keep me standing and got me home.

But it seemed the more time I had to spend indoors, in bed, the more hospital appointments and medications, the more cocktail parties and wedding receptions where I had to explain the miscarriages and our pregnancy journey, the louder my Harbinger seemed to get. Soon, even thinking about my anxiety made me breathless. It was like the memories loomed so large and were so massively painful that they blocked any oxygen from getting to my brain. I could be out shopping, perfectly happy, and I would see my Harbinger and suddenly feel sick, or stoned, or completely dissociated. And like a drunk girl at the end of the night, I would feel desperate to lie down and rest my face on the cold tile, which I did not do, because it is not a polite thing to do in the Gap.

I spent what feels like a good chunk of my thirties on bedrest. It seemed every doctor's recommendation was to lie down for everything. Want to increase the chances of conception? Lie down for a few days. Had a miscarriage? Make sure to put your feet up and lie down for a few days after. Bleeding during pregnancy? Definitely lie down! Pain during pregnancy? Lie down. Had surgery? Lie down, help your body do the work it needs to in order to recover. Had a C-section? Lie down until the stitches are out. Standing up was my enemy and could be a threat to my life or the life of our (potential) child.

Every day seemed to bring another frightening experience that required me to be both frozen in fear and trapped in my own little ice castle of isolation that I built myself. It couldn't be ignored that most of the time when a crisis happened in our life, it was because of something my body did without my brain's okay, and the only cure was to stop my body from moving. My body became a patient, known by a name printed on a thin strip of paper, folded and enclosed inside a plastic bracelet, my traumas displayed for anyone to see, scrawled on a chart hanging at the end of a bed. Repeated over and over again for every intern and resident and nurse. My private places on display for countless people to analyze, diagnose, cut, reshape, and sew back up again. Creating a life was supposed to be a superpower that I held innately within me, but instead my body became a scientific study, a negotiation, and a disappointment.

And all the while, the Harbinger was screaming at me in the background, warning me constantly that if I kept moving forward with this baby train, if I let it run loose, it could take down everything I loved.

Trying to process my response to my fertility journey was a challenge. Because despite the physical pain and psychological trauma, it had been my choice. Looking back at my body after children I can see the scars on my torso, a topographical map displaying the marks from multiple laparoscopic surgeries, two deep cuts on my pelvis from the C-sections, bruises up and down my arms and legs from injections and blood draws. Every mark left on my body — I had consented to it all. I had enthusiastically demanded that we keep trying for children. I paid for this half decade of pain in lines of credit and savings accounts. I had said yes to every operation and biopsy and scope because it had been insisted by experts that they were absolutely necessary. So, was any residual trauma from the experience self-inflected and therefore not valid? If I had listened to my inner Harbinger, could I have saved us from any pain? Did I sacrifice my body for the benefit of our family as a whole, or was

I undergoing this for my own selfish need to be a mother and wield gestational power?

I was also told by other mothers who had carried children that the pain, the memory of the lead-up, and the delivery, fades away after you actually have children. It's true that the first time I saw my daughter smile, a real smile, swaddled and staring at me with the precious crinkle in the bridge of her nose and a tiny blue vein showing through her impossibly soft skin, it disappeared. Her steel-gray eyes recognized me, like only someone who had shared a two-way flow of cells and DNA and a blood stream could, back in the days of my pregnancy when our molecules mingled. I did feel immense pride that I had carried her safely here to our planet despite the dangers. And I was comforted knowing that even as she grows and moves on past needing a mother in her life, the cells that she has left inside my body will be there forever. And I was comforted knowing that I will carry a microscopic bit of every pregnancy before hers within me. And it was true, the only supernatural thing I have ever really known was that the love I felt was like a blinding light so bright it burned away the sadness from the past. And if I had to do all of it again, every single day of the rest of my life, to keep my children in this world, I would. But as the book says, the body keeps the score, and despite the immense joy our children brought me, I also experienced this terrible post-natal anxiety, and my world started to get smaller and smaller. I could keep my Harbinger at bay at home, but that list of places I could go alone without him showing up was becoming smaller. Staring at the fuel gauge, he'd say, "You've got enough gas to get ya there, but getting home, that's another concern." Or lying in bed, he'd pop up and whisper in my ear, "Don't fall asleep, one of them might stop breathing while you are just lying here." Oddly, being in big groups of hundreds or thousands was fine — he could hide in the crowds at the mall, a conference hall, a theme park. That wasn't a problem (there's safety in numbers). Walking in my own neighbourhood was usually fine. But anything new, intimate, or small, any place unfamiliar became terrifying as he would jump around any corner shouting, "Turn back!" or at the buffet like Charlton Heston in 1973's *Soylent Green*, "It's made of people!!" My heart would race, my head would spin, I would feel sweaty or nauseated, and my stomach would get upset.

So I stopped going places. I shut the doors to my castle. I barred the windows. I Iide. Hide. It was safer for everyone that way. And soon the people I loved started wondering why I wouldn't go places with them anymore and why I sometimes rambled when I spoke, going on about my fears, worries, and ancient hurts in a way that probably seemed like I was begging for them to fix things. I think some people assumed I was uncaring or unhelpful or maybe lazy or selfish, when really, I was just a girl who went through a body horror (enough to include a couple of sequels). And like the final girl, I kept tripping the whole way through it, spraining my ankle and throwing myself over a balcony to avoid the explosion; finished it off dragging myself through the mud, clutching an overdue-bill notice in one hand and my car keys in the other, towards my inevitable glass castle of isolation.

Eventually, I started taking medication for my anxiety. It removed the physical sensations that my body was going through, the rigid muscles, the shallow breath, the racing heart. I could go out amongst the living again. But the Harbinger still exists in me, rumbling around in a locked closet in my mind, because every minute life arrives in a series of potential stressors — a kid with strep throat, a messy house, a reprimand at work, car trouble, a sick parent. And he sneaks out to warn me that we are all in mortal peril.

But with my nervous system relaxed and comfortable, I can now speak his language. I make room for him, understanding that for me to fully participate in the world I need to take breaks from it to hear what he has to say. I listen and then say quickly and easily to him, "not today," and steer him back onto doing his basic life tasks. Like, "How about we brush our teeth and fight the inevitable horrors of tooth decay," or "How about we make the bed so later tonight we don't get wrapped up in the sheets and choke ourselves to death." It is a little like we are in an eternal marriage therapy session. "Harbinger, I hear what you have to say about the sky looking overcast, like it could be the seven angels with the seven final plagues bringing on the completion of God's wrath and the doom of mankind, but I would hope that you would also consider my perspective, that it could just be a regular old winter storm and the snow might look beautiful once it's all done?"

It's been a good balance, solid enough that I know how to protect my kids from the strain of my anxieties and help them with their own.

One of my daughters is a real adventurer. She has never kept her two feet on the ground when an opportunity to climb was presented to her. She got stuck in a tree not too long ago. She wasn't very far up. She could probably even jump to the ground on her own, but her fear was palpable. She could not see the way down; which branch to rest a foot on, which burl in the bark was strong enough to hold her, and she was starting to panic. So I did two things:

First, I asked for help. I called over a nearby lesbian couple that I saw holding hands and I asked them if they "had any experience with tree climbing?" They did. And they were only too happy to stand on either side of the tree to spot her.

Second, I had my daughter look me in the eyes, and as I coached her down, I asked her to repeat after me:

I am in charge of my body.

I am in charge of my body.

I know when to hold on tight and when to jump.

I know when to hold on tight and when to jump.

I can save myself.

I can save myself.

I have the power inside of me to find my way out of any jam.

I have the power inside of me to find my way out of any jam.

It is a super power.

It is a super power.

THE HAUNTED HOUSE

(A SPIRITED JOURNEY THROUGH
QUEER HOME OWNERSHIP)

"No live organism can continue for long to exist
sanely under conditions of absolute reality."

— SHIRLEY JACKSON, *The Haunting of Hill House*

It appeared at the time, according to neighbourhood gossip, that my then-wife and I had purchased what would be colloquially known as a murder house. We didn't set out to buy a murder house, but in the wild housing market we bought into, we skipped the structural, electrical, and paranormal home inspection before purchase. In the weeks and months after we moved in, we met our neighbours, some of whom spread rumours with the liberalness one would use to spread buttercream over a cake. *Did you hear? It was sad. Nice guy. Worked hard. So smart. He carried a lot of cash on him I heard. A tragedy. The wife? Oh, she was a tough lady. Fierce mom. Kept a nice home. I bet they would have wanted it this way — not the deaths of course, but to go together.*

We started our hunt across our expensive city, looking for a home we could afford on our modest budget. A fixer-upper.

Something that needed a little renovation, but not too much, and ideally with an apartment in the basement that we could use to cover some portion of our mortgage payment. We had a deposit available thanks to the equity in our one-bedroom plus den condo, and my ex really wanted a project to keep herself busy while I was going through the fertility clinic process. She was worried, though, that I might *actually* get pregnant and we'd have a house to renovate at the same time. My answer was, "Oh no, what if we got everything we ever wanted? Wouldn't that be awful?"

Our agent, a tall, pencil-slim, elegant woman with a short, curly bob and jaunty scarf twirled around her neck, took us to a few homes that were quite run down and immediately rejected. After a month or two of looking, she asked us slyly if we would be okay with looking at some houses that had been on the market for a little while because of . . . how should she put it? Interesting histories.

We talked it over and decided to take a look, because homes are not reflective of what happened inside them, right? Homes are walls, floors, windows, doors, and a roof. Steel and wood. Neither my ex nor I believed in ghosts, although we did enjoy playing around in the realm of the paranormal with visits to psychics, and I read tarot cards occasionally. We were lesbians, after all. I think we both agreed philosophically that we are each given one shot at life; even if you don't get everything done when your turn is over, you don't get to leave a part of yourself behind, floating around afterwards, still participating in the world. That's cheating.

So, based on our shared disbelief, why wouldn't we look for a home with as much bang for our buck as possible? We narcissistically felt the only history that counts in a home is the one we make in it together.

The first House with a History that we saw was a semi-detached on a wide, tree-lined street. Our agent had warned us in advance that an unspeakable tragedy had taken place here, and it had been impossible to sell because of it. A new mother, suffering from postpartum psychosis, had fatally stabbed her husband and one of her children before killing herself, all inside this home. It was the only case of a mother-led familicide in the history of our city. Mothers had killed their children before, but not usually in a murder-suicide, and not usually taking the husband with her.

As we approached the house, we were pleased to see it was much larger and in a far better neighbourhood than we could afford. It looked like every other lovely family home in that area; on a wide street, with plenty of children playing outside. Even with its history, it was surprising that it hadn't sold. Standing on the sidewalk outside of the house was an Italian nonna wearing an all-black dress and sweater set, with thick soled shoes. A neighbour, we assumed. I swore one of her eyes grew significantly larger than the other as she waved her hands at us and said, "No! No!"

We walked past her with a smile and a wave and stepped inside the front door and onto the linoleum tile.

It's one thing to read about a crime, it's another to stand in the space where it recently occurred. What happened in this house was real and terribly tragic. Walking through the family room and kitchen, the air was still thick with grief. A deeply personal kind of grief. Grief that was not my place to be a part of. Like a house on fire, grief clung to the walls and corners like smoke and hovered above us along the ceiling. Someone else would surely go on to buy this home. They would tear it down to the studs and rebuild, I was sure. A new family would probably move in to make a home there, because life goes on. But it wouldn't be us.

The second House with a History that we saw was a little mid-century one-bedroom, one-bathroom bungalow set on a massive picket-fenced corner lot. The huge party-sized deck on the back was almost the same square footage as the house itself. Walking inside, we found the house was empty of all furniture, but some boxes and bags of garbage remained. The floors and counters were grimy, and in the kitchen there was a tarped-over hole in the ceiling right through the roof to the outside elements where I surmised some type of ventilation pipe had been stuffed through for drug cooking. Or perhaps, like at *Grey Gardens*, the hole provided a more convenient entrance for raccoons, a cat door of sorts. Some real estate agents leave out a plate of freshly baked cookies to make the house feel "homey," but this one had left an open box of bullets resting on the cluttered kitchen counter instead. The make and calibre of the bullets weren't displayed, which was wise because one always wants to depersonalize a home when listed for sale.

The walls were yellowed and stained from the floor up with water damage or some other kind of rot. The house was absolutely rank. I won't even begin to describe the bathroom. In short, it was structurally and cosmetically a tear-down. I could envision some very expensive renovation possibilities, with the only bonus being that if it didn't turn out we could lease it commercially as a meth lab.

My ex, however, was spinning in circles with joy, instantly in love. A detached bungalow on a huge lot for under $500,000. This was a property dream come true for anyone in the city who wanted to eventually build something custom. In fact, she was so smitten she had almost put an offer in without my even seeing the house. I put the brakes on and insisted that we have an architect friend take a look to tell us what the cost of renovating would be. We were at an impasse. I could not believe she was even considering this, and she could not believe that I didn't see what an opportunity it was. How could two people with the same vision for our future look at the exact same structure and have such diametrically opposed responses? Unfortunately, or fortunately, depending on your position, while we were arguing, the house was sold to a developer who eventually tore it down and built two townhomes in its place.

The third house was the one we bought. My ex saw the house first and was taken with the fourteen-foot-high ceilings on the main floor and the already established basement apartment. The agent told us that, again, the house had a tragic history, and volunteered with a wincing brightness, "They didn't die *inside*."

The house, despite being in need of significant renovations, with water dripping from one part of the kitchen ceiling and some garish (for our taste) paint choices and worn carpeting, had a good feeling to it. It felt like it was once, and could be again, a happy family home.

Even for this house, which definitely needed work, there was a bidding war. In these times, the fever for a resale home was at its highest. People would buy property sight unseen and pay well over asking. And we were no different, we bought this house for more than we could afford, bypassed all relevant inspections, and handed over a cheque — all before we had even listed our condo for sale. We had never accepted more financial risk into our life than at the moment we closed on this house. But the purchase brought some vigour back into our marriage. We had been working towards a common goal, to have children, and so far that project had been a bust. We needed something new to focus on, and buying a house was a three-storey promise to continue working together to build a future. And as if on cue, a few weeks after we purchased it, we found out we were pregnant again. The strength of the pregnancy was confirmed via blood test and ultrasound on Christmas Eve. We were having a baby. And we bought a house. Everything we had ever wanted for Christmas. We nicknamed the baby Zuzu Petals because, surely, *It's a Wonderful Life*.

But something felt off once we officially moved in. With every bright colour that my ex painted over with her eggshell-white paint, and every inch of blood red carpet she pulled up, the energy of the house changed. Not necessarily for good or bad, just different. For instance, one room became sunnier where I had found it a bit gloomy with its makeshift curtains. That change makes sense scientifically, but it wasn't just brighter . . . If I had to ascribe an emotion to each room, this room would be *happy*. In the hall, where the carpet had been ripped up, *cranky*. Creaky floorboards appeared where there weren't any before, and a cold draft blew through it. A door that used to shut well now seemed to stick a bit to the frame, as though that room wanted to be left alone. The whole house seemed off a smidge, like it had settled a little more closely to the west. But I supposed there was a reason for that too. With all romances, once you start to see the object of your affection regularly, all of their odd bits and pieces start to stand out. A house was likely no different.

When you remove the decorative accents that someone has made to their home, it's like you are removing that person from their own history. If this family were to come back tomorrow, the carpet that their baby took their first steps on would be gone. I imagined that they had long ago argued over the paint colour; she liked orange, and he liked red, so they went with both, with a splash of teal on the side. They were telling us something about who they were with every one of these decisions; the crayon marks that got left instead of being washed off, the newspaper that was curiously stuffed in the walls for extra insulation. They were trying to tell us something about who they were, but we weren't listening. We were intent on destroying and rebuilding.

The reality of our financial situation had started to become more real to me as well. We couldn't move a tenant into the basement until some fundamentals like electrical and plumbing were done. Pregnancy complications meant I had to go on short-term disability leave. We would definitely have to refinance the home to pay for the renovations, so rising interest rates and the amount of our mortgage were storm clouds that appeared to be hovering over only our roof.

I frequently found myself wondering about the family that lived here before. That little hole — did someone hit the wall in anger, or knock a chair into it? Where did they put their Christmas tree? I pictured all of the wonderful things about an urban life that they must have experienced, things that I wanted for my family too. Movie nights and family visits. The homework struggles at the dining room table. The littlest learning to ride a bike in the alleyway behind the house, with a big sister running beside the bicycle the whole way.

It wasn't a fully formed thought until years later, but somewhere inside my curiosity about them was a phantom thought forming. A feeling, really. It was guilt. When we walked into this house, we had wanted some part of this family's life, so we bought it. And even though we paid a fair price for the house, I felt we were benefiting from someone else's tragedy. Our goal was to erase the evidence of this family's existence from what had been their long-time home so we could achieve our own white middle-class dream.

The settler in me feels queasy with this because of the millions of footprints we collectively carpeted over a long time ago in this country, and continue to do so. The places and spaces we marked with our flags that did not belong to us, which we paid for with false currency. Even as queer women, we were privileged in our ability to buy our way out of some of the oppression, while so many others in our community can't. We were able to achieve the dream of becoming homeowners, which is a dream most young adults, particularly queer and trans young adults in Canada, may never bring to fruition.

Queer and trans people leave small towns in droves and travel hundreds of miles to live in cities because that is where they have community and health care and resources and jobs that will support them. They *need* to be here. And yet when they get into the city, they learn quickly that finding housing that has rent affordable enough for them to save up to later purchase a home is impossible. And when housing is predominantly won via bidding wars where the seller can decide which of the potential buyers they prefer, if dollars and cents are essentially the same, people will inevitably choose a nice white middle-class family over radical polyamorous dyke triads or a trans couple.

Home ownership, even haunted home ownership, is an exclusive club, but membership is the only way to find future financial security in our country. Everyone wants *equity*, but it's afforded to only a few. Resale housing prices have been going up reliably my whole adult life, and the security of knowing that we could pull from home equity in a crisis has been the monumental message for having an overall positive outlook in life. Equity is a very seductive concept in all its permutations. It looks like a dream from the outside, but once you get into the work of building it, it seems impossible to retain and perhaps even like maybe it's a fantasy concocted to keep adults doing the painful things. Equity is to grown-ups as the tooth fairy is to children: we will endure any torture, even pulling out our own teeth, for the promise of a little coin tucked away under our pillow in the morning.

Within weeks, there were whispers that something lingered in the shadows of our ancient (for Canada) house that was built back in the 1870s. At first, I told myself to shake off the shudders I would feel when I was walking through the cold spot of a darkened, narrow hallway. I chided myself for acting childishly when I paused before going into the unfinished part of the basement. My heart would quicken, but I laughed at the notion that there could be anything other than solid matter in my home. Soon, however, I began to question my very eyes and ears.

The nighttime knocking in the pipes became an uncomfortable reminder of the expensive work that needed to be done to replace them with copper, and somewhere in the back of my mind sat a memory of the terrifying Mr. Pipes from the show

Ghostwatch, a banned pseudo-documentary that was broadcast one time on Halloween night in 1992. Pipes was a creation of its writers, described as a collection of negative spiritual energy from generations past, a poltergeist who played with the lights, wreaked havoc with the set, and eventually possessed the documentary crew, speaking to the audience through their bodies. The show and Pipes were so frightening that it elicited a *War of the Worlds* reaction across the UK with terrified people phoning in to insist that Pipes had traveled through the airways and into their own homes. The public was so furious that the episode was never aired on BBC again. It wasn't the fear so much as the betrayal of trust. Now, manipulated reality on television is more commonplace than seeing actual reality; we gleefully spoon it up multiple times a day in one form or another. But once upon a time, I want to tell my children (although they would not believe me), we demanded a kind of moralistic integrity from our television programs.

Despite not truly believing in the paranormal on a conscious level, I found myself negotiating out loud with the creepy sensations that I felt in spots of the house. Announcing, "Okay, coming through! Walking down the hall to our bedroom. You don't need to scare me!" It seemed easier to be playful with the nagging feeling that we had potentially gotten in over our heads with this house than it was to actually question if what I was experiencing were real.

Talking outwardly to the spirits of the house, I reminded myself of Eleanor Vance from Shirley Jackson's *The Haunting of Hill House*, although I had always wanted to be like Theodora — confident, beautiful, unapologetically sexual, and able to read people on sight. In the book, these two characters are part of a foursome who are participating in a paranormal research study on haunted houses led by Dr. John Montague and hosted by Luke Sanderson, the heir of the ancestral home in question. Theodora was invited for her psychic abilities, and Eleanor, a shy woman who up until that point had been a caretaker for her disabled mother, was included likely for her empathic nature. By the end, all are fleeing Hill House except for Eleanor, who bonds with the spirits so strongly that she seemingly would rather die and stay as a ghost in the house forever than live in reality.

The Haunting of Hill House is queer canon in literature. Carmen Maria Machado wrote about discovering *The Haunting of Hill House* in an essay called "How Surrealism Enriches Storytelling about Women" for *The Atlantic* in 2017. She said, "The book's particular brand of surreality felt, to me, like that experience of walking home from a party a little bit drunk, when the world somehow seems sharper and clearer and weirder," and highlighted how "being queer, too, can feel surreal. There's this sense that you're seeing things that other people don't, which I think is true of many groups of people who exist apart from the more culturally dominant perspective. You pick up on currents that other people don't notice." To any queer person, reading along as the friendship/flirtation between Theodora and Eleanor progresses, it is vivid and substantial. But to straight people, the lesbian love story at the centre was likely as translucent as the spirits that walked the halls at Hill House.

The section that stuck with me on my first reading was the moment Eleanor finally faces her feelings for Theodora on a walk in the middle of the woods. As their conversation deepens and moves away from how they relate to the men around them and closer to how they feel about each other, Jackson describes the path ahead of them as becoming more dangerous, darker, as its curves and blind spots become more noticeable. But right before they announce their love for each other, they are suddenly met by the ghostly visage of a heterosexual, nuclear family, complete with a puppy, having a picnic. Terrified, they stop running into the dark woods because that pathway is too scary. Hill House seemed safer to them than whatever was down the path they would walk together. Now, I relate more to Eleanor's constant rumination over the hidden intentions of others and her self-damning, fatalistic attraction to holding up the traditional family structure despite her innate queerness.

I often wonder, even to this day, if my ex and I had walked away from the path that was home to a phantom of a heteronormative life, a large home, and big mortgage, would we have become something different? It's why we bought our house after all — I insisted we get married with a wedding and all the trimmings. I wanted to have our own version of a nuclear family with two kids, a dog, and a house with a back yard to grow our family in. Should I have known from the start that this house was not meant for our kind, grabbed her hand and run away?

By the time it was ours, the house we bought had stood for almost 130 years, but I wonder if it will stand for 130 more. Rather than decorate it the way we wanted, we ended up using most of our capital, and my ex's sweat equity, to keep the structure propped up and strong. The floors complained loudly when stepped upon; they creaked like they ached from too many sandings. Doors would get stuck shut. Electricity and plumbing needed to be repaired. Lights flickered. Taps leaked.

There was no insulation, no protection from the elements. All of these things needed to be addressed. The house didn't care about our bills. It didn't care if we froze to death. It didn't care about us at all. It just needed another family in it. Another family to keep it standing for another generation.

Maybe my ex had been right all along with the second house. Perhaps it would have been better to buy something small and tear the whole damn thing down, brick by brick, into pieces.

Maybe we could have built something custom, just for us.

THE HAUNTED

(WHERE DOES THE LOVE GO?)

"I think I can make these Ghosts go away."
"How?"
"Listen to them."

— *The Sixth Sense*

Death comes for everyone. It has a one hundred percent success rate. And these days, divorce isn't far off. Some statistics say four out of ten marriages end in divorce, and the rate is going up with every generation. So when a long-term relationship ends from death or divorce, it shouldn't be a complete shock, and yet it so often is, and we are left in disbelief. There is no screen with big letters spelling out *THE END* when your relationship is over, or a person standing next to your loved one's deathbed throwing up a hand and saying, "And scene," followed by a deep bow. However it ends, you are typically left for a time asking yourself: Is it really over? Did that really happen? And what do I do now with what seems like eternity stretching out ahead, having to rewrite my plans for my future? It's not easy. As they say, life is hard, and in the end, it kills you.

I wrote about living with a ghost post-divorce in the *New York Times*, so I feel like a bit of an expert in the subject, although I am not a Ghostbuster, a historian, or anything of the like. In my case our "ghost" was a reasonable, non-frightening entity who appeared (or rather didn't appear, but seemed) to want to coach me through the more stressful moments of being a single mother to two children. She was a little like a stray cat, too, wandering away at times for months, only to come back when I left something out to feed her. Sometimes, that thing was fear. More often than I would like, it was sadness or stress. But there were nice visits, too, like when my two daughters would clamber upstairs and start cramming Barbies into plastic cars and the family cat into a stroller. That's usually when the lights would flash on and off and my eldest would holler, "Mom! It's doing it again!" And I would reply, "The room is saying hello," and she would yell hello back, and on we would all go with the routine of life. The surprises, the spectacular, the scares, the stress, and the sadness.

Ghosts seem to like routine; in movies and books and ghost stories, they are often stuck on repeat, spectres playing out the moment of their death forever on a loop. The purpose of the ghost is usually to warn of the dangers that befell them causing their death, or to ask for help either in seeking revenge or passing on. But the root of all hauntings is that they want to be heard. Ghosts come from trauma, and they leave the living with residual symptoms of trauma: feelings of intense stress, sweating, panic attacks, and anxiety, feeling numb or frozen. And all of this results in isolation, because those who truly think they see ghosts are often reluctant to talk to others about them lest they be considered mad. Ignore the hairs on the back of your neck. Hide under the covers. Do not speak to, or of, ghosts.

Ghosts are the ultimate introverts of the supernatural world. They've mastered the art of scaring people off just by trying to process their own emotional baggage. Because nothing makes the living run faster than someone stuck in their old traumas. When my marriage ended and I was consumed in grief, many of my long-time friends vanished. I don't blame them. I was trapped in a cycle of reliving the demise of my marriage for anyone who crossed my path. A grieving person is a social reminder of the frailty of human relationships. Few people want to walk the earth alone. Once I had worn out my friend group, I went to therapy to talk it out, but even then I found they wanted to prescribe rather than listen. I took my children to a therapist who wanted them to focus on what was staying the same and what positive things they had to look forward to, instead of listening to them talk about what they had lost.

We demand that the traumatized choose happiness. Cassidy Stay, a teenager whose entire family was brutally murdered, quoted at their memorial service from a Harry Potter book, "Happiness can be found in even the darkest of times, if only one remembers to turn on the light." The message is that being in the darkness of sorrow is a choice and that we can choose to come back into the light of social acceptance whenever we want. The girl's entire family was murdered, and she was already feeling enough social pressure to "choose" to be happy that it was a key message of her eulogy. When I heard that I wondered, have we, as a society, lost our ability to empathize? To sit with someone in their sorrow and hear them. To let them be sad without trying to send them over to the other side. To insist that they walk into the light before they are ready. We consume sorrow from music and film and works of art for hours every day, on the bus or streetcar or sitting in a waiting room or from the audience, but if the person next to us, or even our dearest friend, were to express the same sadness, would we hold them, or would we encourage them to forget their troubles and get happy?

In the 1970s and 1980s, ghost stories typically came in two varieties: fun frolics like *Ghosbusters*, *Beetlejuice*, *Tales from the Crypt*, *Haunted Honeymoon*, and *High Spirits*, or the terrifying epics like *The Shining*, *Poltergeist*, *The Entity*, *The Changeling*, and a hundred iterations of Amityville. But there were a few films that changed the way we looked at ghosts. 1989's *Field of Dreams*, starring Kevin Costner, was a film about a farmer who, like a Midwestern Noah, listens to a catchy message from beyond — "If you build it, they will come" — and creates a regulation-sized baseball diamond in his backyard for ancient baseball playing ghosts to find something to do to pass eternity. Through this act of faith, he ends up connecting with the spirit of his late father. The film raked in the dollars and ushered us into a new period of romance in ghost films.

Supernatural Romance had been a subgenre mostly relegated to vampires, but suddenly in the 1990s ghosts could be sexy, passionate, and deeply romantic. The productions focused heavily on one aspect of grief — longing — and played on the heartstrings of every grieving widow. This was best accomplished in two films: 1990's *Ghost*, starring Patrick Swazye, Demi Moore, and Whoopi Goldberg; and my personal all-time favourite film, 1991's *Truly, Madly, Deeply*, with Alan Rickman and Juliet Stevenson. Neither of these films was frightening or horror-filled. Despite being a blockbuster, there were few special effects in *Ghost*, and they were mostly terrible. But *Ghost* was a sleeper hit and a massive money-maker. It was unexpected because it was initially considered a "woman's film," which usually didn't make bank. But it is still considered a career highlight for its three stars, especially Whoopi Goldberg, who won a Best Supporting Actress Oscar and a Golden Globe for playing charlatan psychic Oda Mae Brown. Oda Mae finds out her power is actually real when she is possessed by the spirit of murdered investment banker Sam (Patrick Swayze) who needs her help to save his distraught widow, Molly (Demi Moore), from the criminals who want to finish the job. Whoopi Goldberg embodies her character with a commitment that is otherworldly. Demi Moore's perfectly placed single tear escaping one eye and rolling down her cheek deserved an Oscar for best timing, and her short, boyish bowl cut lent an extra boost to the heavy eroticism generated from Patrick Swayze's bare chest. Their love scene, with his bulging biceps and thick strong hands reaching around Demi to squeeze fistfuls of pottery clay between her legs, created a communal "hot damn" moment that was burned into cinema history forever. But the scene that really stuck with me personally was when Whoopi as Oda Mae agrees to be possessed by husband Sam so he can dance with his wife one last time. The essence of a man enters into Oda Mae who suddenly becomes something other than male or female. Long red nail–tipped hands reach out to enclose Molly's thumbs, slipping in between the crevices to split them apart and slide inside them. Molly's eyes close, her lips part, and suddenly the audience sees that Oda Mae is Sam. There is more sensual hand action, full lipped kissing of thumbs, before Molly rises before Sam and pulls him to standing. When Sam looks down at Molly, with restraint and longing in his eyes, there is a strong femininity about the way Swayze stands (something we will see Swayze do again in 1995's *To Wong Foo, Thanks for Everything! Julie Newmar*, when he plays a drag queen), and we are reminded that this scene is happening with Whoopi's body as a conduit. It was essentially a possessed, pansexual threesome, and it was super hot. Especially because Whoopi has dodged rumours about her sexuality for decades, despite playing lesbian characters throughout her career in massive films like *The Color Purple* and *Boys on the Side*. And she actively cultivates her queer fandom, saying, "You know, no one was trying to claim me, nobody wanted me. Black folks didn't want me. Nobody wanted me. But I've always been claimed by the gay community. Always."

I enjoyed *Ghost* for the sexy parts, but it didn't touch me in the way that Whoopi Goldberg touches Demi Moore. I think because it is a romance film from a male perspective — a man desperate to continue to protect his woman from danger after he is gone. The film that hit me hard was not even a cinematic release. It was the made-for-TV BBC movie *Truly, Madly, Deeply*, which follows a deceased cellist named Jamie (Alan Rickman) and his translator girlfriend (Juliet Stevenson) who is suffering from what therapists call "complicated grief." Written and directed by Anthony Minghella as a vehicle for Juliet Stevenson, it makes full use of her extraordinary talent and plays her emotions like a symphonic score, taking her character, Nina, from the depths of despair to blinding rage and back up to ecstatic joy all within a few scenes.

I had never seen grief shown in this manner, but I had experienced complicated grief from the ending of a relationship. My first love when I was a teenager was blindingly brilliant for me, and when the relationship ended, as they do when you are a teenager, I was despondent. It hurt so badly and in a way I had never felt before. I had no context for the kinds of emotions I was feeling and no guidebook for how to work through it. The pain eventually subsided, and I went on to fall in love again, and each time it ended in a more healthy and balanced way. But when my marriage ended, I found myself right back in the muck of complicated grief, struggling to move on and constantly ruminating on the loss.

Truly, Madly, Deeply opens with Nina talking to her therapist about how she hears her dead lover's voice constantly telling her what to do — to brush her hair or teeth, lock the back door, walk in the middle of the street when she's alone at night. Despite being surrounded by well-meaning people who care about her and offer her advice, she rejects them, isolates herself, and listens instead to Jamie's disembodied voice. In order to cope with the day-to-day routine of life, she had to manifest his ghost in her mind.

My ghostly experiences started well before the end of my marriage and were not made by my very-much-still-alive ex-wife. Our ghost was an entity that reminded me to do my laundry by spinning chairs laden with clean clothes still to be folded, or to clean up a room after a party by sending balloons to hover over me while I slept. She slid dirty glasses down the dining room table towards us. Knocked photos off the walls that hadn't been hung properly. She was perhaps a personification (can a ghost personify?) of my own anxiety around being a mother and homemaker. She was perhaps a way to keep myself on track. A motivator. The reminder of the consequences of my own laziness.

And then there was that night in the closet when she was a helper. It could have been a scene in any standard ghost movie. I had been living alone for two years at that time and had gone to bed as usual, doom scrolling before plugging in my cell phone and placing it on my bedside table before turning out the light. I woke a few hours later to an enormous *BANG* and was up like a shot. It sounded like something heavy had fallen fast and hard. Half asleep, I waited for the other shoe to drop but heard nothing. I reached for my cell phone to use the flashlight app — not wanting to switch on a big lamp — but my phone wasn't there. I assumed it had fallen to the floor, which was likely the big noise I had heard, so I looked over the side of the bed but it wasn't there either. I slipped out from under the sheets and went down on my knees to look under the bed for the phone, but it wasn't there. While I was pondering where it could have gone, I noticed the door to the closet was moving. Gently. Not enough to open but just bobbing against the frame making a gentle *thump, thump, thump* sound. I had to investigate, but I'll admit, I was frightened. What if it was a serial killer who had dropped his machete and then hidden himself as I awoke? As I walked across the room, I realized with relief the most likely source of the closet door movements — our kitten.

Now, a warning. If you have even an inkling that you may live in a haunted house, I do not under any circumstances recommend that you adopt a cat unless you enjoy the creepy feeling of being watched by an unseen entity, or you get off on catching a dark shadow of something silently creeping about your hallways, seemingly appearing and then disappearing into the ether. Do you want to be the caretaker of a creature that seems unhindered by the physical limitations of the living world, like gravity? Ignorant of all of this, I had adopted a kitten from the humane society a few weeks before, and I laughed at my own shaken nerves when I opened the closet door and she bounded out, glad to be free. But still, I wondered, where was my phone? That's when I saw the light coming from it all the way across the rather large room. On the floor by the door. My phone, which absolutely had been beside my bed, had been thrown twelve feet diagonally across the room where it hit the floor with enough force to shatter the screen, making the sound that woke me up to tell me to help my trapped kitten.

Nina had created a ghost in her mind to ease her loneliness and help her with her nerves from adulting unsupervised. Nina is messy and makes decisions that her relatives and boss and friends all question. Her new apartment is filled with rats and in desperate need of a hundred different repairs. She skips work without telling anyone. Nina has relied on her lover to make her decisions for her for, apparently, years. I related to this as well. In my own marriage, I did not always assert myself in ways that I should have in our day-to-day life. It was part Butch-Femme dynamic, part Virgo-Aries, part six-year age difference, part family-of-origin training. Part undiagnosed ADHD. So when my marriage ended, I felt paralyzed with anxiety over how to manage a house, a car, and not to mention parenting solo when it was my time with our two young children. Soon I found myself out on the front lawn at one in the morning, in my nightie, chiselling ice from the exterior of our air conditioning unit. Or panicking when the upstairs toilet started dripping through a light fixture in the ceiling below it. The overwhelm I felt at this time was very hard to process. Taking one hundred percent responsibility for my own life, after abdicating it to another for a decade and a half, was very hard. Taking one hundred percent responsibility for my own life and the lives of two children was beyond overwhelming. It required me to believe in myself and trust my ability to make wise decisions for us all, something that I had been explicitly told time and again was not my strength. I was at my weakest, feeling the worst about myself that I had ever felt — being left will make you feel that way — and then suddenly I had to be the most responsible and wise and balanced person I had ever been to help steer me and my children through this change.

As part of the complicated grief she experiences, Nina also experiences something called *limerence* instead of love. After his death, Nina overly romanticized her relationship with Jamie. Her desire for him to return is so uncontrollable and so powerful that she actually manifests him into being. Jamie returns to her in the somewhat flesh, to her extreme delight, and they spend the better part of a week making love and getting reacquainted with each other.

But after the bloom of reunification fades, Nina soon realizes Jamie isn't the same person he once was; or maybe he is, but she's just forgotten how obstinate he could be, how self-centred, how much she had to sacrifice of herself to have a good life with him. Jamie brings his ghost friends around at all hours, monopolizing their bedroom VHS player to watch obscure art house movies and their living room to play music together. He is constantly messing with the thermostat. The memory of him was bewitching, but there is little that she finds enchanting about his ghost. So she opens herself up to the idea of someone new when she meets Mark, an amateur magician and social worker for people with Down syndrome. And she finds herself growing attracted to him. They share similar politics and goofiness and a core sense of kindness, while Jamie is misanthropic, cutting, and cool.

When finally Nina has a discussion with Jamie about how she can't go on living with all of his ghost friends, she has an enormous breakthrough in her grief, realizing, "It's life! It's a life I want. And all my taste, all my things — after you died, I found stuff in my coat that I had put there because you disapproved or laughed at. Books and photographs. I couldn't, I didn't know how to light a fuse, or find a plumber, or bleed a radiator. But now I do! And it is a ridiculous flat, I know. But I think I'll get there. It will be beautiful. Could be. And I so much longed for you. I longed for you." But now she doesn't need him any longer. She is enough.

The same thing happened to me. One day my ghost disappeared. And so did the longing I had been carrying around for a life that was no longer mine. I started thinking about what I wanted people to know about me when they walked in my front door, and began decorating my home by buying some simple lamps, a new bed frame, hanging some photos of my family in gold frames to show how much I treasure them. And in the end, I found out that I have my own eclectic, feminine style that I really love, even if it isn't to everyone's taste. With every little (and big) thing that went wrong I started to notice that I can be quite level-headed in a crisis. I started believing in myself, trusting my own decisions, even if they weren't the ones others would make for me. I started hearing my own voice in my head telling me I was okay.

As Mary Oliver asked, "What is it you plan to do with your one wild and precious life?" Will you sacrifice it on the altar of your lost love? Will you vanish along with them? Will you continue to live in the fog of the past, or will you choose your own life? Life is for the living but it's also for the sorrow. Feel the loss, feel it deeply and thoroughly, right down to your marrow, because it is only through loss that we learn the value of something. Just don't stay forever.

In the end, Jamie understands Nina's need to eventually separate from him completely, and he gives her permission and tells her so by reciting a poem by Pablo Neruda called "La Muerta":

> Forgive me.
> If you are not living.
> If you beloved. My love.
> If you have died.
> All the leaves will fall on my house.
> It would rain on my soul.
> All night. All day.
> My feet will want to march
> to where you are sleeping.
> But I shall go on living.

THE STORYTELLER

(MY DAD'S FIRST MURDER)

"You have to be careful with the stories you tell.
And you have to watch out for the stories
that you are told."

— THOMAS KING, *The Truth About Stories:*
A Native Narrative

When I ask my dad what his earliest memory is, he says it's of the river. He means the Red River in Winnipeg, and he's referring to the period of time in 1940 that his family was homeless, his parents and their ten children (with one more on the way). They all shared one tent and an icehouse, "but!" my father will point out vainly, "it was Louis Riel's icehouse!"

Dad is an exuberant and notorious storyteller, with a lifetime of adventures to share, and he has never let the truth get in the way of a good story. This ability to spin a yarn (an idiom that came from women using storytelling to pass the time while winding their threads into yarn) is often met with a mixed reaction from audiences — those who appreciate the distraction from mundanity, and those who feel infuriated by any mendacity. This was explored by Daniel Wallace in his 1998 novel *Big Fish: A Novel of Mythic Proportions* and the 2003 Tim Burton film based on it. The focus of the plot is on a son, Will, who tries to uncover the truth behind his dying father's fanciful stories. The elderly Edward waxes on about his Odyssean adventures traveling with a giant, joining a circus, discovering a phantom town called Spectre, meeting a witch with a glass eye that can foretell someone's death, and the massive catfish that he caught on the day his son was born with his wedding ring as bait. When the son discovers the facts behind his father's tall tales, he learns that alongside the fanciful there was a touch of truth to everything, they were allegorical, designed to teach life lessons.

Big Fish caught my attention because it felt so familiar to me, Dad holding court, telling his tales to new audiences of clients, friends, cousins, PSW caregivers, delivery men, and gardeners. Anyone who crosses his path gets free admission to his show, whether they bought a ticket or not. I have always been of both camps, loving the stories and wanting to follow his yarns back to the balled-up facts.

My father's complete story is a rags-to-riches one that spans from homelessness in his childhood into great fortune, only to lose much of it in the recession of the early 1990s, and to then build his company back up to a nice middle place, with his own children by his side in our family advertising business (an industry ideally suited for someone who loves to embellish the best points and wash away the least desirable facts). Now in his eighty-eighth year, many of the facts of his life as they stand are inspiring. He picked up ice mountain climbing at seventy-five, scaling several mountains that year (without a helmet because it would muss his full head of white curls). He went to Simon Fraser University in 1968, when he was in his thirties, the year the Students for a Democratic University took over the school, campaigning to rename it Louis Riel because, as they said in their manifesto, Simon Fraser was a "member of the vanguard of pirates, thieves, and carpetbaggers which dispossessed and usurped the native Indians of Canada from their rightful heritage." Dad was there studying political science with a minor in African studies so he could better support civil rights. He and my mother went so far as to join the Peace Corps in 1969 and were settled on moving to Africa, a plan that was only stymied when my mother found out she was pregnant while getting her vaccinations. A staunch feminist, Dad always paid women equally and put them in positions of power in his company, and he is still always very eager to point out the superiority of the female sex to my sister and me. He used to flip the Saturday paper open for me when I was a child and say, "Okay, kid, show me one violent crime here perpetrated by a woman. *One*. Find me one, and I'll give you twenty dollars." But perhaps best of all, he was devoted to my mom whom he met in Winnipeg when they were in a split grade one-two class together. They were best friends for over eighty years. In a story that puts *The Notebook* to shame, my mom developed a degenerative brain disease called multiple system atrophy, and Dad cared for her body and soul every day for twelve years: doing her hair and makeup, taking her out for walks in her wheelchair, claiming to everyone he met that "she's on drugs, I'm her pusher." By the end of her life, she couldn't really talk anymore. But that was okay to them both. He always did most of the talking anyways, regaling her with stories of his past adventures. One of which he calls "My First Murder."

Back in 1952, Dad and Mom used to run a weekly dance for teenagers in their local community centre. Mom did the bulk of the work, and Dad was the emcee. They had a band and a dance floor, punch and decorations, and a little stage, and Mom and Dad would sing and dance together as entertainment. I can picture them there, Mom with her short auburn ducktail haircut and bright blue eyes, slipped into a nice respectable dress with a full skirt and bolero jacket, a belt around her impossibly tiny seventeen-inch waist. Dad in the one black suit he owned, his tie the only thing in the room skinnier than him, a pocket square peeking out, his curly black hair cropped close.

One of the adults chaperoning the event was the editor of the *Winnipeg Free Press*. He liked my dad's energy, knew he was graduating high school, and offered him an internship at the paper with an agreement to mentor him. My dad was eighteen years old, and his first day of work at the newspaper was on June 29, 1953. He remembers, because no sooner had he unpacked his bag than his mentor was calling him into his office. "Sit down, Chuck," he said. "I'm afraid I have some bad news. Your father passed away. You'll need to pack up your things. I'll drive you home to your mother." My grandfather, who worked construction, had, a few days before, accidentally hit his head on the grader machine he used to build roadways. Without CT scans, the hospital had stitched him up and sent him home, but there was an unseen bleed in his brain that had grown. His sudden death left my grandmother a widow with five of her eleven children still living at home, the eldest being my dad and the youngest being only eight years old.

My dad went back to the paper the next day with a different purpose now — to financially support his family. To help, the newspaper had given him an additional evening overnight shift and use of the car. His job at night was to listen to the police scanner and attend any crime scenes that took place to take notes for the reporters. Then at 2 a.m., he was to go to the local bar, pick up the "seasoned" sports reporters, and drive them all home to their wives.

He says he felt like a man for the first time in his life instead of a boy and relished this experience. He had a car! He was the man of the house! As the fairly flamboyant middle child between seven hyper-masculine brothers and three sisters, he believed he was the one in charge now, and he felt this way until the night of his first murder, when everything changed.

Dad remembers sitting in the car, parked on the side of the road in a rough neighbourhood, listening to the police scanner, when a voice rang out looking for a unit to attend to "a body on Vernon Street. Is anyone near Vernon Street?" Dad held his breath when he realized *he* was on Vernon Street. And sure enough, as he drove slowly up the street, the headlights of his car revealed the body of a dead man lying in the snow with a knife sticking out of his chest like a cross. No one was around; the streets were entirely empty, except for my dad and this body. The only sound was the rumbling of his car engine and the static from the police scanner. Dad slowly got out of the car and walked through the slush and snow to the crime scene where he stood, silently, over the body of a middle-aged white man, and watched steam rise into the cold air from the gaping wound in his chest. There was no breath coming from his mouth. No movement, no signs of life, no dramatic sprays of blood. Just a dead body, in the snow, with a large knife stabbed straight into its heart. Dad stood there, taking it all in. And he said he suddenly felt very, very young. Like a little boy. And he was scared. What the hell was he doing here amongst this horrible violence? Was the murderer watching him right at that moment from one of the nearby houses? Would he rush out and stab my father too? Would the murderer remember his face and come after him later? Or, maybe even worse, would the police arrive and think *he* was the murderer? How would he explain this? He panicked. He ran back to his car, made a wide U-turn, narrowly avoiding a snowbank, and took off. He drove onto a side street, turned his headlights off, and waited for the police to come. The End.

I can picture my pop, standing there over a dead body in the coldest hours of a Winnipeg winter night — one of the most unforgiving places in the world to experience winter. But there was an important part that he never mentions in his story — the identity of the victim. Who was this man out late on a snowy Winnipeg street, and why had he been so brutally stabbed and left for dead in the cold? And so, like William in *Big Fish*, I set out to find the hard facts of my dad's tale, weaving his fanciful yarn like a police detective does on their corkboard, attaching the pieces of his story that I knew to be true to potential players or details.

I pored through all the crime reports in the newspaper archives in Winnipeg from the general time period. I read about every stabbing, and I found a lot. A ton of stabbings, actually. But not one case that sounded *exactly* like what Dad had told us: a white man murdered in the winter via stabbing where the body was found lying on Vernon Street.

Researching his story made me question something else he had told me that I had accepted as gospel about women and violence. I found some astonishing stories about crime in Winnipeg in the early 1950s, and perhaps most shocking to my worldview at the time was that the majority of them were perpetrated by women.

A forty-one-year-old immigrant from Hong Kong murdered her physically and verbally abusive husband who often threatened to divorce her and deport her and her elderly father, whom she cared for in their home. The night of the murder, her husband had come home drunk and physically assaulted her, in a way disturbingly described by the reporter as "chewing at her hands." She stayed calm after this assault and for the rest of what was to come that evening. She cooked a late dinner and fed it to her husband. Then she helped him get into bed, climbed on top of him, and stabbed him in the chest.

I also uncovered the case of a young husband who was seen staggering aimlessly up and down his street with a knife still sticking out of his shoulder blade. Not quite the case my dad described, and this man survived. He wandered the street for over an hour before the police were called. When they finally tracked down his wife, she said she didn't understand what all the fuss was about. She described it as "an ordinary little fight."

There was another man who was stabbed in the chest that same year by an ex-girlfriend. He had been stalking her for two and a half years. She had gone to the police repeatedly and even moved three times trying to hide from him, but he always found her. One night he saw her at the local legion hall and followed her back to her rooming house suite. He broke in through a window and assaulted her. While he was choking her, she managed to manoeuvre them backwards towards a kitchen counter where she reached behind her, grabbed a paring knife, and stabbed him to death. I thought maybe it was him, but he died in the rooming house, not in the street.

For all my research, there was no man with a knife in his chest found dead lying on the freezing cold streets of Manitoba in the winter of 1952 or any time around then.

I'm not saying it didn't happen. Perhaps my research wasn't thorough enough. Or perhaps it did happen, but my father didn't file the story because it had upset him so greatly, so this man's death went unreported. Just one more stabbing in a long line of murders and assaults in a city that was still reeling from a horrible tragedy. The Red River flood of 1950. That's a story we don't hear much about, although it most assuredly was a traumatic experience for Dad and his entire family.

That flood was Canada's largest evacuation in history at the time. Over a hundred thousand women and children were put on trains and shipped north to cabins and cottages, while the men and the navy stayed back to try to protect what they could. There was water up to the rooftops in huge swaths of the city. Mass destruction to the tune of tens of millions of dollars. Thankfully, only one reported death during the flood; but no one counted the deaths that happened as a result of the post-traumatic stress. The people in the city of Winnipeg suffered enormously after that natural disaster with homelessness, joblessness, and environmental health concerns that most certainly wouldn't have been dealt with to today's standards.

So, I'm left with two options: either my father has conflated more than one story, and it didn't happen the way he said it did, or this victim's story was lost to history by not being told in print. That's the thing about storytelling versus journalism. Amplification and embellishment are helpful when telling great stories, but there are times when facts are essential — dates, times, locations, and names — frequently, the dullest parts. But we miss the totality of the story when the telling of it centres solely around facts. We need the impact, the emotions, the drama and danger, the perspectives of the people involved. We need a balance of both to tell the story in full: enough facts to build trust and enough embellishment to entertain.

I think if I were to *Big Fish* this story and look at it as an allegory or a metaphor, a lesson for life, the core that reveals itself is that my father, a young man just about to begin his adult life, had to face how senselessly, carelessly, and quickly death can come about. His own father, a vital and strong man, who wrangled eight sons and physically built the roads in Winnipeg, was killed by something as mundane as bumping his head. Dad barely had time to think about the trauma of that loss because he had to get to work immediately, and here he was faced with another middle-aged man whose life was extinguished suddenly, stretched out on one of the roads his father had probably built. My father was undoubtedly a witness to trauma. And like a nesting doll, trauma begets trauma, which begets more trauma. Reporting crime, consuming crime, researching crime, even telling crime stories, creates a new (although much smaller) trauma for the listener and the teller.

Some traumas are so big that they won't fit up on a shelf or in our curio cabinets. Some are so big we have to carry them with us 24/7, which can be awfully heavy, so we turn them into stories that are easier to share with others and take some of the load off ourselves for a while. We make them entertaining so they are less likely to traumatize someone else.

In *Big Fish*, Edward passes along a list of qualities he respects to his son which include perseverance, ambition, personality, optimism, strength, intelligence, and, above all, imagination.

Imagination is the act or power of forming a mental image of something not wholly perceived in reality; a creation of the mind. Which, incidentally, is also what a memory is; the faculty by which the mind stores and remembers information. A creation of the mind, born when specific neurons are locked into place in a certain sequence. Like the old electronic game *Simon*, the more times you activate that sequence, the stronger the memory becomes. But over time, that memory or a portion of the memory inevitably fades and disappears. But because of something called synaptic plasticity — the ability of our brains to create new synaptic connections — we can replace the ghostly remnants of a memory with something else, something we can easily access, a synapse that we know well, like a symbol.

Our brains are constantly patching up our memories like our favourite pair of jeans, just so we can wear them out again. The more time that passes, the more pieces of the memory that fade and are replaced with symbols, the more recounting a memory can become like sharing a dream than a factual retelling of a moment in time. Some memories are so powerful and emotional they light up our amygdala, the fear centre of the brain, which makes us more likely to remember those unsettling events. That's why Dad remembers that story — because it was a powerful moment in his life. And also why he doesn't remember it in perfect crystal detail, because a moment in time becomes a memory, which then becomes a fragment of a memory, which then becomes a dream, and, finally, becomes a story told for generations. But none of the stories — my grandfather's death, the kindness of the newspaper editor, how talented and sweet my mother was, the drunken newspaper reporters, the man in the street who was left alone to die, the women who turned to violence, the people evacuated in the flood — none of them are ever truly forgotten once they become a story.

Because now you know them too.

THE TEENAGE GIRLS

(SATANIC PANIC '92)

> "Dear diary: My teen angst now has
> a body count."
>
> — *Heathers*

S pring of 1992 had come in all its confused splendour, almost ready to pack away another cozy Canadian winter, but not quite ready for the brilliant summer heat. We were two years into this new decade, and the PR message was that we were an entire planet on the edge of incredible peace, prosperity, and wellness. The UN had declared 1992 International Space Year to "highlight the importance of understanding Earth as a complex, interdependent system in a vast universe." It was hard to understand why alongside this message of safety and security being broadcast on all now thirty-plus available TV stations (including a twenty-four-hour news channel), were more sinister scenes like IRA bombings, brutal civil wars, military coups, and struggles for independence across the globe. Things did not look peaceful. Even right at home, Leslie Mahaffy's body had been found less than a year earlier encased in concrete in St. Catharines, an hour's drive from us; and a long way away in Martensville, Saskatchewan, over a dozen people, including police officers, were accused of running a secret satanic pedophile cult called The Brotherhood of The Ram out of a daycare centre.

Canadians were completely dumbfounded by that revelation. Child murders and satanic cults were so . . . not Canadian. Our global reputation was one of peacekeeping, deference, mutual care, and easygoing natures. Could there be such evil lurking in the places we consider safe, like a local daycare centre in the middle of rural Canada? There was a CBC radio contest that once asked listeners to send in an ending to the aphorism "As Canadian as . . ." The winning answer was ". . . possible, considering the circumstances." Were we not what we said we were? Could evil people exist in Canada?

In 1992 I turned eighteen. A flaming confection was spread out before me, eighteen candles. I remember closing my eyes, allowing a series of childish fantasies to run wild through my imagination. Choruses of "make a wish" filled the air, when I heard the voice of my steadfast best friend Jane rise above the fray with a warning to "BE PRACTICAL."

Jane was a good girl. In her worldview, nothing you possessed, even a wish, was to be wasted. She and I had been close friends since we met at an Anglican church Sunday school as toddlers, despite being two different sides of a coin. Jane had grown up to be fit, studious, and disciplined, her long straight light brown hair usually pulled back in a clip behind her big curled bangs. She wore simple slacks and peach or mint-green pastel sweaters and listened to pop music and '50s classics. Jane didn't drink or smoke and wasn't going to have sex until she was in an established relationship that looked like it was going to go the long haul. Jane was going to become a teacher. She had set a plan for her life, and everything was going to go according to that plan.

I suppose some would say I was the bad girl, in comparison. I was an outspoken, emotional, and persistently love-sick high school girl. I wore short skirts and black clothes. I listened to Depeche Mode and The Smiths and bypassed the hairbrush for hand-scrunching my curls into huge fistfuls of mega-hold gel like Bad Sandy after her makeover in *Grease*. I was going to university to get a degree in theatre so I could "become a professional Drama Queen," as the joke went. Even my major seemed childish and impractical. I drank too much Molson Canadian, smoked du Maurier Light King Size, and had sex with my boyfriend in the front seat of his K-car, sometimes doing all three simultaneously. I couldn't even wait to get into the back seat. If we were characters in a horror movie, Jane was the final girl, and I was definitely getting murdered topless.

We rounded out our group with two other best friends: Sherri, who was bold, creative, and hilarious, a bouncy goofball, but who could also be very thoughtful and insightful in a Janeane Garofalo kind of way; and Karen, a slim, shy, piano-playing, cat-loving, outdoorsy girl with a secret naughty streak. At the time of my eighteenth birthday, we were in our final months of high school. Acceptance letters to universities were arriving in the mail, and the four of us, who until now had been together every day for years, were going to three different schools. Sherri and I were the only ones staying together. We were going to be moving into dorms or apartments with strangers and, like in the brand new MTV show *The Real World*, expected fun conflict, new romances, and adventure.

Up until this day, our lives had existed within a protected white middle-class bubble, carefully constructed both for our comfort and to keep us quiet and contained so we could be entertainment for others. Even though it was the '90s there was still no question that we would all go to university or college, get married, have children, and lead decent lives. But with university looming, our protective bubble appeared to be thinning. Just three years before this was the École Polytechnique massacre, but that was a freak occurrence, a madman. And the disgruntled associate professor at Concordia University in Montreal, who had just shot and killed four colleagues and wounded another, was another bizarre but isolated tragedy. Leaving home to go to university was still an exciting prospect. Besides, we weren't going far — all of our schools were within a few hours of home. I don't think we could have imagined anything farther than our provincial boundaries at the time.

At eighteen, all I wanted to do was drive. I had initially been nervous to get my licence, but once I was behind the wheel I was in mad, passionate love with the power and freedom it presented, and I almost always drove us anywhere we went. Jane usually rode shotgun because I picked her up first from her little bungalow with the English country garden on the corner, with a wave to her British Mum and Dad, her father hollering after us, "Don't do anything I wouldn't do then, yeah?" Then I would head a few houses down to grab Karen from her simple, neat, and tidy, almost identical bungalow. Karen was always waiting at the bay window for us, playing a Sarah McLachlan tune on her upright mid-century piano, slipping out quietly so as not to disturb anyone in the house. Finally, I would make a quick right turn to where Sherri's family lived in a two-storey with a swimming pool out back. Sherri was always ready with a prop or practical joke for the evening, a dismembered plastic hand from Halloween stuffed into her purse, "Oops, don't want to forget my handbag!"

Driving my friends was a bit of a break for my mother, who, although she sometimes complained of being nothing more than a taxi service, *never* wanted me to take the bus. At first, I wondered if she was being classist, but then I realized it was more likely because of the stories that had been appearing in the news about girls, as young as fifteen, being beaten and viciously raped by someone who apparently had followed them from bus stops in nearby Scarborough.

My mother didn't say anything about it outright, because I think she knew if she had I would have rolled my eyes at her fears. Being attacked by a rapist seemed as likely to happen to me as a man with a hook for a hand climbing through my bathroom mirror. But I was grateful for her generosity in allowing me to use the family car.

The minute I turned off the highway and onto the winding rural back road that connected our small town of sixty thousand people to the closest urban centre, Scarborough, I would pick up speed like the devil was on my tail. Faster and faster I would go on the straightaways, not slowing down much to account for the curves and the darkness. Shooting through the forest and out past the fields, faster and faster, feeling like the huntress Diana in her moon chariot, blazing across the sky. With windows open and curls flying, I would race down this familiar back road alongside bucolic farmland. In a few years, this area, like all of the rich and fertile farmland in our town, would be bought, severed, dug up, and converted into housing developments. New communities designed for my friends and me to move back into, to raise our children. But not tonight. Tonight, the road was our empty playground, and I could open up the engine and put my high-heeled foot to the floor while Jane tapped on the console saying "That's enough now, Allyson, slow down," Sherri sang along to the CD, and Karen giggled in the back.

The car was a black 1990 Pontiac Grand Prix, known for its high-tech computerized console that was like something out of *Star Trek: The Next Generation (TNG)*. You could control the volume on the CD player right from the leather-wrapped steering wheel, and on the warm spring night of my eighteenth birthday we had the moonroof open and windows down and we were all chair dancing and singing to George Michael's "Freedom! '90": a song about trying to transform lies into truth and how we feel ownership of the people we covet.

I loved this iconic queer anthem and the David Fincher–directed video that heralded the beginning of this new decade. The lighting, which years later we would refer to as bisexual lighting, was all German expressionism, that deep mysterious blue, with tinges of pink, heavy on the shadows. While various supermodels, in the time it takes them to boil a kettle, languidly lip-synch his confessional, about how the road to hell can sometimes be confused for the road to heaven, Michael came out to the world while hiding his face from us. The song was an apology to his gay fans for previously masquerading as straight, and it offered a commitment to tell his own story from here. But I didn't really understand any of that at the time. I just vaguely knew it was his coming out song. I did notice one scene in particular though, the only one with the models not in isolation. In a series of strobe-like flashes, Christy Turlington and Canadian Linda Evangelista make a bi-implied, teenage-girl pact, pricking their fingers with a needle and rolling on the floor together, suggestively biting their lips and sucking on intermingled bloodied fingertips. These bi women weren't hiding in their closets, they were rolling around inside them wearing gorgeous sweaters. The video said something to me about how even in secret places like your own bathroom, your own bedsheets, the places you are half-naked and vulnerable, you are always, first and foremost, queer. And that means you are never alone, because, like the Borg in *TNG*, we are a collective consciousness. We can recognize other queers through our gaydar.

Of course, hiding and being invisible are two different things. Hiding is fear-based, but invisibility can be a superpower. At least that is what I was contemplating at the time. Because I was scared to make my queerness visible to my friends and the world, afraid I would scare them. My bi-ness was not supermodel beautiful to me yet. I was afraid they wouldn't understand. I wasn't interested in Linda Evangelista, I was already swooning over pictures of a shaven-headed Ripley in David Fincher's next project that was coming out a month later in '92 — *Alien³*. And it was a love that was growing desperate to burst out of my chest.

"I think there's something you should know, I think it's time I told you so. There's something deep inside of me. There's someone else I've got to be."

I didn't notice the car following behind us until the spinning blue and red lights popped into my rearview out of the darkness. It was like they came out of nowhere. No headlights. Nothing. I unleashed a tirade of profanity as visions of groundings and expensive tickets and maybe even losing my licence all flashed before my eyes. I had never been pulled over by the police. Was I going to be arrested? A uniformed man got out of his car and greeted me by shining his flashlight through the window, blinding me momentarily. I averted my eyes from the glare, my hand trembling as I fumbled for my driver's licence. For all of my faux-girl-power-bravado moments ago, I caved in the face of male authority. I was clearly no bisexual Catherine Tramell, flashing her feminine power like a middle finger at the police in *Basic Instinct*.

"How are you ladies doing this evening? Where are you headed to?" He shined his flashlight into the backseat, and I could finally see his face. A young man, younger than I expected. Maybe not that much older than we were — in his twenties maybe? Shaggy-on the top blonde hair. Wearing some kind of uniform, but no policeman's cap. "I was speeding," the confessions instantaneously spilled from my lips, "I'm sorry. I'm sorry. I'll slow down."

"That's okay," he chuckled, fairly informally for a police officer, I thought. "Hey, is this a Grand Prix?" he asked, reaching his hand in through the window, inches from my face, and stroking the dashboard in front of me. "I, ah, always wanted to see the inside of one of these." He chuckled again.

Sherri's voice came loud and strong from the backseat, "Can we see some identification, Officer?" I was sure she had definitely landed us in jail. "Oh my God, Sherri," I chastised her. "He has lights. You can't pull someone over if you aren't a cop. There are *rules*," I said. He angled a sly smile in my direction, and there was a long, tension filled, awkward pause before he confessed to us, "Actually, I'm a security guard."

My stomach dropped straight through the chassis and onto the road. I had experienced boys trying to get my attention before, but this wasn't the same. This wasn't a guy whistling from the sidewalk. This felt like . . . an ambush. What if I had been alone? Had he been following us? Did he see a car full of young girls and follow us with his lights off, waiting for a dark road to pull us over? Hadn't Ted Bundy pretended to be a police officer?

Despite being at the wheel of a V6 engine, I didn't drive off immediately. I sat there like a chump for a minute or two as my emotions circled from fear to anger. When I did pull away, he didn't follow us. He stayed there, perhaps waiting for the next car of girls to drive by, enjoying the moment of control he had exacted over us. We didn't report him. We would have had to find a pay phone and look up where to call in a phonebook, and then we would be late for dinner and the guy would be long gone. The whole experience seemed absurd. Sinister and absurd.

We tried to put it out of our minds and enjoy a fun birthday dinner at my favourite 1950s-themed diner, eating french fries and drinking slushies, putting quarters in the tableside jukeboxes, waiting for our songs to come on. I felt just like Baby in *Dirty Dancing*, but hopefully without the abortion and rape. I had almost completely forgotten about the security guard as we headed home, until I automatically turned back onto the road he'd stopped us on. Despite my trepidation, it was still the fastest (and most fun) way to drive home. I drove the speed limit this time.

The road wasn't empty as I had expected, even considering the late hour. We were being followed closely by two sedans. Way too closely. I sped up, assuming they simply wanted me to go faster. But the car behind me matched my speed and stayed glued to my bumper. With nowhere convenient to pull over, I sped up again. The car behind me made a sudden swerve to the left and passed us clocking probably ninety or a hundred klicks and shot off ahead of us into the night. Now the second sedan behind us replaced him right up at my bumper and flashed their brights at me, blinding me in the rearview. To this point, it just seemed like a couple of kids being jackasses. They were probably street racing and my car was in the way.

That's when I saw ahead of me that the first sedan, which had jetted off a minute ago, had now come to a dead stop, sideways, in the middle of the road, like a police roadblock. Across the entire narrow road. I slammed on the breaks, the ABS making a *click-click-click-click*ing sound. Gravel dust rose off the roadway. The girls shrieked, bracing themselves for impact. The car behind me swerved and by some miracle avoided colliding into us. All three of our cars were now at a standstill on this dark, narrow roadway. One sideways blocking the path in front of me, the other now diagonally blocking the lanes behind me, my car sandwiched in the middle.

I immediately honked my horn in outrage. Inside my car the air was thick with upset over this idiot. "He could have killed us!" I lay on the horn for a few seconds more, but no one made any indication that they were going to move. Had his car broken down? It looked like it was still running. I impotently honked the horn again to no response.

Slower than it should have, the realization hit me that we were trapped on this stretch of roadway. My car was blocked in on all sides by either cars or trees. This front sedan had stopped at this spot for a reason. I tried to back up, to turn and go the other way, but the car behind me would not budge. This was no accident, the two cars were working together. *This* is the ambush, I realized. Someone piped up, "Oh my God, is it that guy? The security guard?" No, we all agreed. It couldn't be. It was a different car for sure. For sure. Right?

Jane took control, assuring us that the front car would move in a second and we should all stay calm. As the seconds turned into minutes, we scrambled for answers as to why two cars would block us in on this pitch-black road in the middle of nowhere. Did we recognize the car? Was it someone we know playing a joke?

And then Sherri wondered out loud what we had all been thinking. "What if it's a cult? This area has been known for satanic cults. They do ritualistic sacrifices out in the fields." Karen agreed, "It's true! People's pets have been going missing for weeks. I think they steal cats and use them in the sacrifices. It's not always babies."

"It's not Satanists," Jane said, always the voice of reason.

"You don't know that, Jane. It could be!" I screeched, siding with Sherri and Karen on this one. Sherri then gave us a brief but informative lesson on the history of the Manson Family from her independent study research for Society, Challenge and Change, her thesis being, "See, Jane, even if it isn't a satanic cult, it could still be a murder cult."

You could say we were being hysterical teenage girls, but since the Salem witch trials, the term *emotional hysteria* has been a marionette thread between reasonable teenage female anxiety and emotion, and the people who utilize them for control. We may laugh in retrospect at the panic that led us to think supernatural occurrences were the real threat to us that night, but the stereotype of a screaming teenage girl exists because teenage girls have valid reasons to scream. What really scares society is the idea that teenage girls are uncontrollable when they scream together. And maybe that's not such a bad thing. Girls need plenty of healthy opportunities to scream together in fun so that when we need to scream in outrage or fear, our voices are prepared.

I remember looking up at the moon, which was about halfway towards full, waxing gibbous, and I was thinking about those anonymous young girls from Scarborough who were being followed home by someone and brutally attacked. I felt deeply sorry that I had not paid more attention to their stories. I was also intensely grateful for the privilege and security of the reinforced steel around all of us and the power locks. My eyes burned a figurative hole in the tinted windows of the driver's-side door of the car in front of us, waiting for what I expected to happen next, which was that the interior light of the car would switch on as the door opened and a car full of long robe–wearing devil worshipers would drag us by the hair out of our car and into the fields. I would be nailed to an upside down cross for my secret obsession with wanting to run my palm along Ripley's shaved head, or Sinéad O'Connor's, maybe Annie Lennox's.

Maybe the Satanists would forgive me, actually, being absolutely devoted to evil sexual impulses. I didn't know much about Satanism, but I knew Christianity preached social conformity — *stand up, kneel down, follow my rules, forgive those who hurt you, especially if it was us* — whereas Satanism was said to promote hedonism, freedom from authority, and bodily autonomy. It's no surprise when I look back on it now that what turned out to be false accusations of satanic cults were often against day-cares, right at the same time that women were pushing back on authority, establishing full on careers, and needed the support of those daycare centres to improve their circumstances. Those empowered women must be evil.

Maybe the devil worshiping cult would take my perverse, women-loving self in? We saw it in *Bram Stoker's Dracula* (also released in 1992), the three brides of Dracula are shown as wanton, insatiable bisexual sluts. And by the end, pious Mina and libidinous bi Lucy have both, of course, become demonic creatures having given in to carnal lust. That's what freedom and bisexuality gets you — a one-way ticket to hell, with non-stop French kissing along the way.

Back in the car, after an excruciating five minutes passed, the headlamps on the car in front of us snapped on and the car made an awkward six-point turn and started moving ahead slowly. The car behind us started moving as well when we did, but at a respectful distance this time. My friends and I audibly exhaled with relief that this was over and immediately began filling in the empty places of understanding with excuses for their behaviour. Sympathy for the devil worshipers. It was probably simple car trouble. Maybe the driver had lost control and hit his head and needed to rest? Maybe he was drunk? Maybe we should have gotten out to check on him?

But our peace lasted only a few hundred more feet. As we reached the next curve in the road, the car in front did it again. He swerved to the left and blocked us in. We all screamed. Someone in the car started crying a little. It might have been me. This was no joke. Whatever cat and mouse game they were playing with us was certainly not going to get any easier on us this next round.

I looked to level-headed Jane, who was scanning the area, looking to the woods on our left and the farmer's field to the right. I read her thoughts and unleashed. Pedal to the floor, the car lurched off the road and into the field. I zoomed around the Satanists and fishtailed back up onto the gravel. I drove as fast as I could get the car to go until I came to the main highway. I knew that this moment was the zenith of my friendship with Jane. Her level-headedness and my risk-taking abilities behind the wheel combined to save us from what was most certainly an awful death on a makeshift pentagram on the ground.

The next morning, I caught hell in the church parking lot when my mom commented on the muddy state of the Grand Prix. But I don't think I told her about the cars and the security guard and the certain death. Whatever actually happened on that dark roadway, stayed on that dark roadway until now.

The week after our satanic panic, a girl was walking alone through a church parking lot in St. Catharines when she vanished. An inverted fairy tale, her penny loafer was the only thing left behind to show she had been there. And strangely, a torn fragment from a map of Scarborough. The first time I saw the abducted girl's face, the air seemed colder around me. The streets were awash with real killers, not just fantasy ones. And the person who pulls you over on a dark road really could be one of them.

We were changed by the horrific disappearance of Kristen French. This girl we didn't know but who looked so familiar. From the photos sent out by the police, she resembled my best friend Jane. They had the same bangs — rolled under with a curling iron and teased and sprayed on top. Her halo of brown hair was nicely scrunched into waves, likely with a white cloud of L'Oréal Studio Line mousse. She looked like a lot of the girls at my high school, actually. I bet she played French horn in the school band, or the flute, I thought to myself. And ringette, I bet she played ringette. She looked like she could be kind of sporty, I imagined. She was pretty. She probably studied. She definitely didn't smoke. We all held our breath for two weeks. Her body was found in a ditch along the side of a road. Her long chestnut hair shorn off. Police told us to be on the lookout for a cream-coloured Camaro.

It was around this time the riots started in Los Angeles in response to police brutality against Rodney King, a graphic incident that had been caught on camera and broadcast worldwide. The officers had been acquitted, with the judge saying the beating, which caused permanent brain damage, had been a "reasonable expression" of police control. At a peaceful protest against police brutality in Toronto on May 2, 1992, a young Black man in Toronto named Raymond Lawrence was shot and killed by police officers when he approached them, and the riots started here. Reporters called it a "seething sea of humanity," and over the six-hour duration a hundred stores were looted and damaged, thirty-two people arrested, and dozens injured on Yonge Street. The majority of the rioters and looters were not people of colour, but young, white men. Mostly skinheads, apparently. Yonge was called "Fear Street" on the front pages. But the people we were supposed to fear right now, apparently, were Black people, not the police, nor the neo-Nazis whose behaviour had been the purpose and cause of the violence and destruction, and definitely not Satan worshippers or serial killers.

A few weeks after the riots, I was back at the wheel with the girls heading to Karen's family's cottage for Victoria Day weekend. No parents, just a dock, a lake, a canoe, and some board games. I probably snuck some Bartles & Jaymes Light Berry coolers into my bag along with my du Maurier King Size. We chair danced and sang: "This here's a story about Billy Joe and Bobbie Sue. Two young lovers, with nothing better to do. Then sit around the house, get high and watch the Tube. Here's what happened when they decided to cut loose." Behind us, a cream-coloured sports car pulled up to my bumper, and then quickly passed us on the left. "Was that a Camaro?" I asked.

"Pay attention to the road," Jane reminded me, "and slow down."

We didn't call anyone about the Camaro, either, and the police eventually caught Paul Bernardo, the Scarborough rapist and serial killer of Lesley Mahaffy, Kristen French, and Tammy Homolka, along with his willing accomplice, Karla Homolka. They did it without our help. He didn't even drive a Camaro. They had been so close to catching him so many times, but I don't think the police were ready to believe a duo like them could exist in our little corner of the world.

Like the rest of the planet at this time, we claimed to be a country on the brink of a decade of promise with new space-age technological advances that would bring us more peace, prosperity, and inclusion than ever. But Canada as a (colonized) country was still rooted firmly in its adolescence in the 1990s, searching for a national identity that was unique from our neighbours to the south. We tried on a hundred different outfits, hoping to find one that fit us right, and even it if wasn't authentic, it would be one that would make everyone happy, and not seem too threatening or too out there — something practical. And the persona that we landed on was: Canada is safe. Canada is kind. Canada is welcoming. Canada protects its children. Canada doesn't have psychopaths.

THE PREGNANT WOMAN

(CONCEIVING FEAR)

"This is no dream! This is really happening!"

— *Rosemary's Baby*

"**W**hat colour is my wallpaper? Yellow. Obviously," I said to myself, aiming the tiny arrow to the centre of the word *yellow* and selecting a floral virtual background template for my WordPress blog page (that I would soon abandon). I felt it would be better for the bedsheets if I worked on a laptop, instead of my preferred method of pen and paper, because I'm prone to falling asleep mid-sentence and waking up in bed sheets stained with ink. Truthfully, there wasn't much else for me to do while I was languishing in bed "with child" on another round of bed rest for subchorionic hemorrhaging, the medicalized term for heavy bleeding during pregnancy. With my history of recurrent miscarriages, it was necessary. At any point, if I moved around too much, I was told the chorion membrane (whatever that was) could dislodge, causing another miscarriage. The OB/GYN said this with a surprising lack of gravitas — almost casually — for a diagnosis so filled with potential horror on my part. But I guess when it comes to their job, what we consider horror is to them routine.

My non-marching orders were clear: I was not to leave the bed except for short sojourns back and forth to the bathroom. Brief showers. Sometimes I felt like a petulant child who had been sent to her room to "think about what she has done" — being a lesbian and getting knocked up. Not too long ago, I had been flying high with the news that I was pregnant again, and shortly thereafter I was grounded in the reality of my predicament. Tasked double with the weighty responsibilities — to both create a healthy and viable human life in nine short months using only my uterus (by far the coolest thing any of my organs have ever done), and also to control what seemed uncontrollable simply by staying still. No pressure! Literally. I wasn't to put any pressure on my stomach; I had to lie on my left side when I slept and not roll over onto my front. I tried to think of ways I could control what my body did when I was unconscious by building myself a small fortress of strategically placed pillows, but short of someone tying me to the bed like in *The Exorcist*, I had no idea how to prevent stomach sleeping. Although, being restrained like Regan seemed appropriate given that my body seemed to have been taken over by an unseen force dedicated to wreaking havoc on me and my unborn child.

Well-meaning folks told me to relax, enjoy the break from work, and pointed out how lucky I was. "You won't get much rest once the baby comes," they would say with a ribbing elbow. I typically replied with a self-deprecating one-liner, "Lying in bed all day watching TV — I've been in training for this my whole life!" But frankly speaking, I was crystal clear on one thing — that as a woman, keeping my body under control was my one job in life, and I failed at it miserably. It has been all at once frightening, shameful, and embarrassing to me, having others witness how unruly my body has always been. I was even born with crooked legs and had to wear corrective braces attached to my shoes while I slept until I was two. I guess I should have always known I was never completely straight.

Early in my fertility journey, I had been given an early 2000s copy of *What to Expect When You're Expecting*, a pregnancy guidebook, although parts of it could have been written by Stephen King, the master of describing all manner of terrors occurring in what heretofore seemed like a normal neighbourhood. Round ligaments felt more like the curved blade of a mezzaluna knife than simple elastic tissue. Lightning bolt–like shocks to the vagina made me imagine a tiny Dr. Frankenstein inside me, pulling the baby up by its umbilical cord to get a jolt, yelling, "It's alive!"

The cover art on *What to Expect* was a twentieth century Rockwellian illustration of a woman, big with child, wearing a rose-coloured muumuu while resting in a rocking chair and holding a book, which we are to assume is this book. The pages of the book she is holding are blank, but if we could see the cover art on the book she held, I imagined it would be her holding this same book, the recursion on the cover getting smaller and smaller. Ad infinitum. Truthfully, this cartoon woman chilled me to the bone. She rested from her place on my side table with one hand on her baby bump and her eyes on me. Her mouth sliced straight across her face, slightly turned down on the sides; it was hard to tell if her expression was emotionless, wistful, or sad, but one thing was clear: it was not the wide, happy smile of an expectant mother that you would expect if you were expecting. Every time I looked at her I thought to myself, this lady knows something, possibly everything, and it's all inside the book. She was the gatekeeper to gravidity.

The book, although helpful, did the opposite of calming any fears I had about being part of a high-risk pregnancy. Opening that book was like pulling the hockey mask off of Jason Voorhees — you might get the answer you're looking for, but it doesn't change the inevitable terror of your circumstances.

Pregnancy is terror, you say? Isn't it the most beautiful time of a woman's life? In my experience, it was both things at the same time. Stephen King famously said in his book *Danse Macabre* that horror is the moment at which one sees the creature, while terror is found in the suspense. Not that the sweet baby is a creature, but so much of pregnancy is suspenseful. For those of us blessed with anxiety and wild imaginations that are hard to put fences around, there is no limit to the scenarios we can conjure in our minds, or even feel in our bodies.

Because pregnancy is one of the only times in a person's life that is truly filled with *actual* suspense, if you give a person a chance to talk about their pregnancy, which is of course a natural and life-affirming process, it's often like they are recounting the details of a true crime story. There is of course also the body horror of watching your own form become unrecognizable, ballooning up in the front, red and purple stretch marks appearing on your limbs and belly, feeling your bones and ligaments stretch and separate, noticing subtle changes as your liver relocates up next to your heart and your stomach and intestines get squished together. Your blood volume increases.

Parts of your body that were dormant suddenly awaken, like your mammary glands. Like *Invasion of the Body Snatchers*, the Pregnant Woman experiences a loss of bodily autonomy and the intrusion of another human being sharing your torso. All with the threat of something going horribly wrong resting on your shoulders. And by the end of my first pregnancy, I had spent the better part of three quarters of a year on bedrest, with nothing to do but contemplate risks. I died in ten thousand gory scenarios I concocted in my mind before the eventual safe and sound birth of our perfect and much beloved child.

I live in a relatively safe country with universal health care, but all uterus-owning people will be familiar with the stress of having reproductive health concerns be pushed aside by doctors. We know we can't always trust that when we go into the place where we are most vulnerable — like the birth process — that everyone there will keep our wishes, and birth plans, up front.

Even though it's rare, many of us have heard stories of those who died or became disabled during childbirth. Stories that aren't ancient history. Statistics Canada reports that 523 women died from complications of pregnancy or childbirth between 2000 and 2020.

I had a neighbour who was raising her granddaughter after her daughter fell into a coma as a result of complications during a C-section. The last time I spoke to them, which, granted, was years ago, the mother was being kept alive on life support indefinitely. The child had been told her mother was like Sleeping Beauty — an age-appropriate explanation. A woman frozen inside the moment of birth, feminine and fragile forever.

Pregnancy exists in the realm of miracles, which is why it's perhaps the most complex and controversial aspect of human life and frequently explored in art. The pregnant person in film and literature is a dark spring night. Both mercurial and wise, she is a study in opposites. She was only yesterday a damsel in distress and not yet the all-knowing mother. Seen as being both a monstrous personification of body horror and an angelic Madonna. There is power in her vulnerability — rise and give her your seat! Make way for the pregnant lady! — and she is clearly a sexual being by way of her situation, but she is now off limits. She is an adult who must be protected as we would do a child, at all costs, by those around her.

The pregnant woman is always portrayed as the easiest to dupe. Pregnant women in classic horror have minds that are as transmutable as their bodies. And like Rosemary in *Rosemary's Baby*, they are susceptible to implantation of any thought from sketchy doctors, abusive husbands, or your co-op's devil-worshiping cult. She will consume anything and everything suggested to her by suspicious doctors and "helpful" neighbours. The paradox is that she is fragile and needs help, yet she is also capable of creating another life, which makes her powerful.

During pregnancy, this life she's creating is only visible to us through the dramatic exterior changes to her body. With birth, we are able to finally see how the baby has survived inside our bodies, this child who is both beloved and parasitic. The pregnant woman also illustrates the repulsiveness of our insides to us. During labour and delivery, the woman takes what was on the inside and pushes it through great pain and force to the outside — blood and bodily fluids, sticky membrane sacs, a pulsating umbilical cord, and a meaty placenta. And if you are having a C-section, this is all revealed by a scalpel while you are awake, which sounds like something from *Hostel* or *Saw*.

I've been through this myself with two C-sections, and I still feel woozy on contemplating it. It still seems surreal to me that twice over I lay on a table, awake but paralyzed, with half of me covered by a sheet while I was cut open by a doctor, like a dark magic trick, all while my partner watched. And then a live baby was pulled out of my body. And I survived that. How is that possible?

When we look at the pregnant woman through our ancient brains, we assume she is slower to respond to a threat. She can't run as fast or jump, so she must be weak. But anyone who has been pregnant knows the extra hormones during this time make your claws lengthen faster and become less prone to breakage. Your hair becomes lustrous, thicker, and if you were on bedrest like I was, you let it grow like cavewomen did because it protects you from the cold. Your joints become more supple, more flexible. Your body changes for the better in many ways. But as a society we don't like body change. Other than the natural aging process, which is acceptable to fight, or adding implants to make us more sexually attractive, bodies are allowed to change in only two ways — smaller through weight loss, or larger through weightlifting. *Any* other change has proven frightening to the masses.

On one extreme end of this continuum is the transphobic social rejection of masc women, non-binary people, and trans men who either want to experience pregnancy or find themselves pregnant by accident or abuse. It flies in the face of our number one rule — protect pregnant people at all costs. How can we as a society protect the same people that we target? "Think of the children!" Conservatives cry. They struggle to accept the sheer audaciousness of someone walking around, living their life, creating new future-tax-paying citizens, while needing access to safe healthcare and public bathrooms, all while looking different than the woman on the cover of *What to Expect When You're Expecting*. As though children being born to self-actualized, brave, introspective people who *want* children could be bad.

For me, I was outwardly what society is most comfortable with for pregnant women. I was fragile and feminine, stoic and determined, hidden away from view, mostly frightened but dealing with it. I was dedicated. I wanted our child so much I would literally endure becoming a gothic horror novel trope by spending seven months in a potentially haunted house on bedrest.

I tried to distract myself from the torment of my incapacitation by keeping my mind active. I attempted knitting and found I was terrible at it. I watched classic Stephen King–based horror movies like *Misery* and *Carrie* and *Cujo* and *The Shining*. I read Neil Gaiman until my eyes nearly bled. I painted my nails. I practised putting on liquid eyeliner so I could look like Anne Bancroft in *The Graduate*. Sometimes I felt like a broken-down doll living my life in that room, mostly alone. But every day I put on a new dress and some makeup and wound my opera length pearls around my neck, because they have always been good luck to me. I waited for anyone to come upstairs and knock on my door. Take me out to play.

Being alone in one room for months on end was tedious and anxiety-provoking for someone with an anxiety disorder, but I had no other choice. So, I sat there in a comfortable purgatory of my own making.

Because I can definitely say at that time in my life in my early thirties, I was doing exactly what I wanted — participating in the rites of passage and rituals of modern life, even if I was queer. *Not* having a child simply wasn't an option I was willing to consider. Who would I be if I did not get married or become a mother? As a stable adult with a well-paying job, a supportive partner, a house, and a puppy, it was the *obvious* next step.

I had wanted to be The Pregnant Woman, with the baby showers and the summer maternity sundresses, and yet on bedrest I found myself frightened in so many ways by my pregnancy that I was rarely able to actually enjoy it.

When I did have occasion to dream about the future with the baby in a positive light, it was glorious. After all, a marriage is not about the wedding and being a parent is not about the pregnancy. I always believed that someday a little being would join us, bringing joy and love. And then she did. When she arrived, I had all of the good feelings, a love that was bigger than anything I had ever experienced, just like the books said I would, a perfect little baby who slept with her head nuzzled into the crook of my neck. And then her sister came with her astonishing blue eyes and fierce little temperament. And like I had been told to expect, the fear I experienced in my pregnancies, the pain, and the sorrows all vanished like a cloud of baby powder into the air.

I think I gained a different perspective on terror in my situation. I now look at the terror of being pregnant and in jeopardy more like the gothic writer Ann Radcliffe first explained in her posthumously published 1826 treatise *On the Supernatural in Poetry*. Radcliffe wrote that terror is found in obscurity and the resulting horror is sublime. She posited that *beauty* could be found in the experience of both terror and horror. Radcliffe suggested that terror "expands the soul and awakens the faculties to a higher degree of life." In other words, limitless creative potential is born of the number of scenarios our mind's eye can build, and horror is sublime, a word meaning "beyond all measure." Horror can transcend the mortal realm, becoming something that we could not ever possibly conceive, even with all our potential creativity.

Sublime has, in modern times, become contextual with the beautiful, but long ago, the sublime was often considered a mixture of pain and pleasure. Philosopher Edmund Burke said in 1756 that the sublime is "a sort of tranquility tinged with terror." Arthur Schopenhauer referred to the Fullest Feeling of Sublime as being the moment that we understand and take pleasure in the immensity of the universe's extent from our simultaneous nothingness and oneness with nature, which could destroy us.

And what better exemplifies that than the experience of birth?

THE FORTUNE TELLER

(PLAYING THE CARDS YOU'RE DEALT)

"Where there is tea, there is hope."

— SIR ARTHUR WING PINERO

D o you want me to tell your fortune? Read the lines grooved into the palm of your hands? Run my thumb along them, feeling for minuscule breaks in the lines, lines that only I can detect? Trace the branches as they intersect with each other, connecting your fortune and your future or, in most cases, your head and your heart?

My paternal grandmother was a scryer, which means "one who divines the future." She read tea leaves and tarot cards and knew a little palmistry. But she died long before I was born. Our relationship never existed in flesh and blood, only in story. So instead of futures, I find myself trying to read her past to see where I can divine some guidance.

I've been told on occasion that my energy is similar to my grandmother's. But having never met her I can neither confirm nor deny any similarities beyond the deep marionette lines I see in old photos of her, signs that we both liked to talk a lot and built strong jaw muscles. I'd like to think I am as resilient as her, as capable of navigating through hardship.

Her mother was quite possibly Basque, her father was a Scottish-Canadian CN Rail worker who died in an avalanche in Revelstoke, BC while trying to dig out a buried train. We actually have a letter from a man who was standing near him when the snow slide hit, but who survived. He said my great grandfather was a very brave man. CN Rail disagreed and said he was a "volunteer," and since he wasn't technically working that day, his wife and their thirteen children were not entitled to either death benefit or pension, which were only to be handed out to the workers who died on the job. He wasn't even entitled to a grave. Instead, destitute, his family was divided and sent to live apart from each other all across Canada, from British Columbia to the East Coast. My grandmother lived for a time in Montreal before eventually finding herself in Winnipeg. A wife to Walter Scott, and a mother to twelve children, of whom eleven survived and one who died as an infant. She was pregnant and nursing her entire adult life, while raising her children, each born a little over a year apart. No twins. My grandfather was a labourer who worked long hours for little pay building roadways. They were extremely poor. Every morning she woke at 4 a.m. to stoke the woodstove in their tiny two-bedroom, uninsulated home in Winnipeg. Every morning she would shape and prepare either a large pot of oatmeal or a tall tower of two dozen cake doughnuts for the family breakfast. The older boys would be up by five to do their paper routes, lifting their winter coats off of the younger children, which unfortunately was what they used as blankets. Soon, shivering and cold, the youngest ones would wander out of their bedroom rubbing sleep from their eyes to warm up with a hug. Then she would get the children off to school and spend the day doing their family's washing in a tub on the floor of the kitchen, which might also substitute for a bath later. There was no running water in the house, no indoor plumbing. She cared for the children all day, and then she stayed up late, until my grandfather was home, to keep the fire burning. She likely never experienced a full night's sleep in her adult life.

Her husband insisted that she have a full day off from children and home duties once a month. On a Saturday afternoon, she would hop on the trolley car that stopped in front of their house and ride down to the local movie theatre, where she would buy a sandwich at the Woolworths counter and then head in to watch a nickel matinée at the Vogue theatre. On the trolley ride home, she would plan out her performance. The family didn't have much, but they had one extraordinary, highly coveted luxury — a piano. My aunt Margaret, elegant and lithe, would play and sing while my grandmother would act out the entire film for the children, and sometimes the neighbours, who would come by to visit. She would bring all of the music and mystery and magic of the big screen into their tiny house with her. Eventually, my aunt got a job playing piano and doing acrobatic dance before the movies, and my father worked as an usher, ticket taker, and eventual assistant manager of the theatre as a part-time job while still in school.

Some nights they would lend the piano out to other families who were having a party; on those nights, the neighbourhood men would come over and haul it up onto the back of a pickup truck and drive it down the street. On Sundays, my grandfather would plow driveways and trade for extra food. Sometimes it would be enough for a roast beef dinner, which was always thinly sliced and shared with other families struggling through the harsh economic times in the late '30s and '40s in Winnipeg.

It was a chaotic, stuffed-to-the-brim, but happy and peaceful home. The only violence my father remembers is when the eldest boy in the family, Earl, lied about his age and tried to sign up for the airforce to fight in WWII but was sent home. Determined, he went back a second time to the navy recruiting station but was again sent home. He finally went back a third time and was accepted as a motorcycle messenger in the army. My grandmother sobbed and beat him with a broomstick. When he decided to marry a girl he had just met while he was out on the East Coast for training, she got on a train and dragged him by his ear to the courts to have the marriage annulled. She needed his war benefit to keep the family going. One-by-one, all of her sons joined the air force, or the navy, or the army, and the young ones joined the cadets back at home. They took to calling themselves Grace's Army. The sound of a bicycle bell ringing on the street was enough to make her feel faint, because it was the bike messenger that brought the telegrams to the mothers of those who had died.

When she worried, which was constantly, she looked to her cards and tea leaves. But, for all her divination abilities, she couldn't see the exact tragedy that would befall her family. She only knew that it was on its way.

If her family had stayed in the Basque region, my grandmother may have been called a sorginak, the Basque name for witch. And she may have practised the Akelarre, a Witches' Sabbath similar to one celebrated by the followers of the Greek demigod Dionysus, women who would run naked through the mountains drinking and celebrating without men. As a lesbian, this concept intrigues me. I likely would have been called a witch myself if I had lived at any other time, for my love of cats and my curly reddish hair alone. But Grace's family didn't stay in the Basque region, and she wasn't a witch, she was a mother. She worried. And cared for others. And worried more. And the worry and the stress led to high blood pressure, which led to a stroke that she had in her early forties and survived. Afterwards, she was confined to bed, enclosed in a metal cage around the top of her body because the weight of the sheets caused nerve pain that was too much to bear; but with time and physical therapy she got better, and soon she was walking and back to caring for her family. The cage remained, though. Her youngest daughter, Danielle, was the only one who was small enough to fit inside it with her mom, so she slept in the cage too. Every bed had at least three people in it.

The next tragedy that struck, when It came, came quickly. My grandmother had traveled to New York City to help her eldest daughter, Margaret, with her first child. She stepped away from her duties at home and enjoyed the sights and sounds of the most cosmopolitan city in the world. While she was there, she received a telegram from my grandfather saying he had hit his head quite badly at work, but no matter, she was to enjoy the rest of her holidays. She knew something was wrong and boarded a train immediately, making it back in time to say goodbye. He died soon after from a bleed in his brain caused by a workplace accident. Another workplace accident taking another father, but this time Grace was determined that the family would not be separated like her own family of origin had been.

Grace may have been widowed with several children still at home to care for, and no identifiable skills beyond excessive procreation, but she had a skill. There was no real work-from-home opportunity in 1952, so she became a fortune teller, reading tea leaves and tarot cards for local housewives. Divining meaning from the shapes left in wet tea leaves isn't in use much anymore, but essentially it works in a similar way as tarot cards do. You direct energy and reflect your intentions into the loose tea leaves left over in your cup, and by looking at the shape, density, colour, and placement, one who is trained in this type of divination can foretell your future.

Neighbourhood mothers would descend on her kitchen for a cup and the latest gossip. As they sipped on their tea, they would set their intentions — their spirit would transfer into the leaves. They would watch her hold the cup in her left hand and swirl the dregs of liquid in the bottom of the teacup three times, from left to right. Then, ever so gently, she would place the saucer on the top of the cup and flip it upside down, holding her palm to the bottom of the cup. When the energy struck, she would turn it again three times and then lift the cup back upright to reveal the message. "Hmmm . . . tsk-tsk . . ." She knew all their secrets before they could open their lips. Affairs, resentments, pregnancies, troubled children. She knew it all.

Her psychic readings kept them afloat until the day Mrs. LaPorte sat down in front of her. My grandmother uncharacteristically stopped the reading mid-way. "Let's take a look at a different cup," she said, and began preparing the ritual again. My grandmother had seen something awful. Death. Sudden, painful, horrible death. Mr. LaPorte was going to be taken from his family quickly, and soon. My grandmother wanted another chance for this woman to have a better fate, a different fate than her own. But she knew she couldn't make any changes to this scenario, as no matter what she said, the ultimate fate laid out in the bottom of the cup would still take place. Death cannot be avoided. All she could do was pour another cup of tea. Mr. LaPorte apparently had a massive heart attack the next day and died, and my grandmother already had some food packed up and ready to go for the grieving family next door. She put her fortune telling away for good after that.

When I was a young woman, I was intrigued by tea leaves, but I found it a little like trying to find the constellations. I enjoyed the search for symbols and meaning in the chaos, but I couldn't quite see the pictures in the dots. I preferred story-telling, so I went with tarot, following their original use as storytelling cards. One person would flip over the Lovers and begin a story about two lovers wandering through a garden, and then the second might turn the Hierophant card over, and the mystery would begin, until the fated Death card appeared and the story ended.

The idea came to me when I came across my brother's vintage pack of 1973 James Bond 007 *Live and Let Die* tarot cards amongst family games. The bright yellow box peaked out from underneath a copy of National Geographic like Charlie Bucket's golden ticket, with a psychedelic illustration of a dapper Roger Moore on the front, his gun erect, and the sexy Solitaire draped over his shoulder. I assumed my brother wasn't using them — as far as games were concerned, fortune telling was for girls, and Risk was for boys. These were going straight to the next church rummage sale, I surmised, and selling them at a church rummage sale would be sacrilegious because reading tarot is a pagan ritual. In this way I rationalized pocketing the deck that was not mine to own as a good Christian thing to do. I took the deck back to my cement blocked dorm room to teach myself how to read fortunes from the handy-dandy instruction booklet. Inspired by my grandmother's resourcefulness and a need for free alcohol, I decided to try reading tarot cards in exchange for drinks at my university pub.

As a person with multiple privileges, I see now that fate is a word happy white people use as a universal explanation for why good things seem to land in our laps. Accountability is not what most people want — most people would like to be cradled when the hard times fall or when the tough decisions must be made. They want someone else to tell them what is meant to be or why something happened. Fortune telling offers a nurturing calmness, a way of saying, "This path was set out before you long before you came. Your ancestors built the pathway with stones from the graves of their ancestors, and somewhere in the universe an angel blessed your birth and foretold your coming. So, yes, yes, yes, you should definitely quit your analyst job at the insurance company and take up pottery."

As a queer person curious about psychics and readings, I pay attention to films where there is someone in the role of mystic or fortune teller, as it has always read as exceptionally High Femme to me. The clairvoyant is theatrical, feminine, dangerous, but also nurturing and someone you can trust with your deepest secrets. She will hold your hand, stare deeply into your eyes, all the way into your soul, and she'll tell you that good things are coming your way. Be patient, but keep going. And when times are rough, you can be assured that she will break the news gently: "You're in danger, girl." When it's a woman, she is your best friend, a secret lover. Even when it's a masculine character, he is always a little bit femme: stylish, strong, brave, sensitive, willing to suffer a little for the greater good.

The clairvoyant is camouflaged. She looks like all of the others, which allows her to watch from the fringes, mostly an outcast, but not entirely. Not allowed to fully participate in society, yet she understands human nature better than most because she is able to see it from the perspective of another dimension. I prefer the stories that are told from the perspective of the psychic, often exploring how painful it is to be the person who bridges two dimensions, like we see in *The Sixth Sense*, *The Shining*, *The Dead Zone*, or *The Green Mile*, to name just a few. The psychic is often someone who has experienced a great trauma, or a life of abuse and neglect. Unseen, oppressed, othered. Finally, something triggers their powers, and we all discover that, internally, this person had a great gift that they weren't sharing, a secret. A hidden ability akin to a superpower, that they could have used to hurt, or for their own personal gain, but they chose to help others instead.

I don't consider myself psychic, but with all of my readings, I became attuned to people asking the same question over and over again. Am I going to be okay? It didn't matter what the question was. "Does he love me?" is just another way of asking, "Is he going to break my heart? Will I be okay?"

Reading cards was a bit of a rush for me. I could forget my own worries for a while and focus on someone else's. It required me to be quiet and listen to someone and connect with the energy they were giving off both physically and emotionally. I'm not a small talk person, I have social anxiety, so at that time, in university, I would usually either clam up, ramble on, or start kissing someone. Reading cards gave me a reason to be in the room, an opportunity to step away from the social stress, and focus deeply on one question at a time. I think because I am a decently empathetic person with performance training, I could effectively match the energy of the person in front of me. In drama class, we learned how to transfer energy between people in a way similar to the way a choir harmonizes or a band plays together. Synching energies with someone helped me understand the answer they wanted, or what was keeping them from the result they sought. Were they anxious, nervous, sad, despondent, desperate, exhilarated? Reading their emotions was as much a part of reading cards as the cards themselves. That isn't to say I was being dishonest — I wasn't — or that I think psychics are flim-flam — I don't. Like all professions, I am sure there are a wide range of people with different sets of values, ethics, and beliefs. I was absolutely reading cards, but I wasn't doing it by drawing on forces from the universe, I was taking a complex question, a bundle of emotions in front of me, and finding context by focusing on the symbol on the card, the meaning that had been ascribed to that symbol in my James Bond 007 *Live and Let Die* tarot card training manual.

When it comes to myself, now, even though I hold the cards, I still can't help but ask the questions. Am I going to be okay? Will my little family be okay? Will this ever get any easier? Does she love me? Is this love sustainable? Is it real? Is it responsible? Is it the kind of love you can raise a family on? I want the comfort of those answers. The older I get, the bigger the consequences of making the wrong decision seem to be. Because far from being alone in the world, at some point in the last five years I have realized how deeply interconnected I am with my family and friends. If anything were to happen to me, or to any of them, it would have a ripple effect across our whole little ecosystem.

Life is filled with insecurity around the potential negative consequences of our choices. People will cling to any faint wisp of an answer, and when you put your questions to a psychic, for a moment in time, someone else is not only bearing witness but supporting you in your fears. They are partnering with you on solving your conundrum. It's slightly maternal, very intimate; many people choose visiting a psychic over seeing a therapist.

One way or another, sharing our decisions and looking at the consequences of life are necessary, because free will is too big of a concept to cope with. Nothing about the future is carved in stone. It's a fact right now, that across the vast expanse of the entire known universe, we are the only sentient life force. And we will likely never know if we aren't. We also cannot possibly know with one hundred percent certainty if there is a heaven, or if reincarnation is real, or if nirvana exists. We will not know if an afterlife of any kind exists until it's too late to tell anyone else about it. So if we believe we have one life, and we believe we are alone in a vast universe with infinite possibilities ahead of us and only a finite number of days, how could we *not* get overwhelmed by making even the smallest decisions. Jean-Paul Sartre, the philosopher who unpacked what responsibility means to humankind, said, "Man is condemned to be free," meaning that with ultimate freedom comes an impossibly heavy burden. If we cannot from time to time lay our decisions down on the shoulders of someone else, how can we possibly bear the weight of them?

Thankfully, we'll always have our own way to connect the past and the future as one, because as Arthur Dent says in Douglas Adams's Hitchhiker's Guide to the Galaxy series *And Another Thing*..., "At the centre of an uncertain and possibly illusionary universe there [will] always be tea."

THE CRONE, THE MAIDEN, AND THE RACCOON

(TRASH CONVENTION)

> "The way I see it, every year can be a brand new
> journey. Think about it: You get one chance
> to be 25, 38, 44, 61, and every age before and
> between. Why wouldn't you want to experience
> all the wonder in each step on your path?"
>
> — OPRAH WINFREY

Sometime during the spring of our first year in our haunted house, while I was mid-way through my pregnancy and confined to bed, I began hearing noises in the walls of our bedroom. The sounds typically started in the early hours of the morning. A *tap, tap, tap*ping. Occasionally, it was a slow dragging sound followed by a *thump*. Small footsteps. Scratching, constant scratching. It was The Ghost, I assumed, naturally. She must be stuck in the walls and trying to claw her way through the wallpaper to come and get me, like in Charlotte Perkins Stetson's seminal feminist work *The Yellow Wallpaper*. "Rodents are more likely," my ex said. "A raccoon. Maybe squirrels. Hopefully not rats." Surely it was the fault of the "slumlord," a woman who owned the seemingly abandoned row house attached to our freshly painted home, bustling with new life. Her house was so run down it was inevitable that something from there would make its way over to us here. Like having a conjoined twin with scabies, we were bound to start itching at some point. Looking out the window at her property was a constant reminder of the entropy and neglect that comes with an aging property, when all I wanted to focus on was my beautiful new life.

I was growing fond of the room I was spending all of my time in, with its high ceiling, immovable king-sized bed, the unevenly dark stained subfloors with thick splotches like cleaned up blood pools, and four tall, thin windows. I enjoyed watching the sunlight change colours as it streamed through the stained glass during the different hours of the day, making shadows on the walls in the same sort of formless figures that clouds make.

If you were to take an inventory, our neighbour's decaying backyard was full of the following: four-foot-tall ragweed, creeping charlie, and fleabane; wrappers and cans discarded by passersby; the partial skeletal frame of an abandoned bicycle; a toppled chair that appeared as though it had passed out after a rough night, its torn upholstery looking like its skirt hitched up, exposing skinny legs; a heavily mildewed tennis ball; and plastic water bottles containing cloudy liquids. Every window on the main floor was barricaded with wood. It looked as though the apocalypse had taken place on that small square of land but someone forgot to tell the rest of us.

The only regular visitor to the house was the owner who would occasionally be seen creeping around the yard with gloves on or in the back alleyway. And every few months, an airport taxi would pull up out front and a bright young international student would step out eagerly holding their suitcases before the inevitable look of horror after taking in the state of the house that they had likely rented based on catfished photos seen online back home in Korea. They never stayed long. The longest group of renters, I think, was the Nocturnal Drunken Irish Footballers League who enjoyed the place immensely from the hours of 11 p.m. to 4:15 a.m. every Thursday through Sunday.

The house was a tall brick Victorian, identical in structure to ours, but where ours was painted a contemporary gray with a postage stamp-sized concrete pad out front, hers sported ribbons of peeling red paint and an overgrown wild rose bush out front that spilled out over the fence and onto the street. More thorn than flower, it used to frustrate me to no end how the thorns would grasp at my skirt when I walked by as if to yank me back into the yard. But it had been months since I'd set foot on the sidewalk, having been on bedrest for so long now it felt almost normal to exist mostly in one room. I could still see the rose bush from my window, though, when I pulled my blinds up to look outside. In the centre of the gnarled mess of vines, flashes of yellow goldenrod strained to break out.

We called the fire department about the house once when an alarm went off. We were worried about squatters, which I think now we call phroggers. The firefighter suggested we leave it alone and not make a formal complaint because, at best, the house would be condemned and nothing would change for years. At worst, we would have a war on our hands with our neighbour, and nothing good comes from war. What harm was her house really causing, he suggested, other than being an eyesore and attracting occasional vermin.

The owner of the house next door was a petite, fit, older woman who, from what I could surmise, could have been either fifty-five or seventy, her age completely impossible to determine based on her innocuous style of timeless baggy jeans with T-shirts and her perpetual scowl. She had long, bottle-dyed hair that she pulled back tightly at the front but allowed to spring out into a frizzy ponytail at the back. Her voice was unusually high-pitched, thin with undertones of gravel and violin strings wound too tight. She was the only regular visitor to the house and could occasionally be seen padding around the backyard, picking at things but never making much headway. She didn't live in that house — she owned several rental properties, and this was likely her least favourite based on the amount of attention she paid it. Sometimes she would do bigger renovation jobs that never seemed to actually get finished but would happen alongside our never ending reno.

On breaks and after a day's work, our friends would sit on milk crates in what my ex called Garage Mahal, and smoke cigarettes. Next door her men would do the same, sitting in a haze of cigarette smoke on her makeshift front porch, which was basically a platform made of plywood. Her men would pitch their butts one-by-one into the brambles of the rosebush, and I would watch judgingly from my tower window, sure a cigarette would ignite the house at any time.

It wasn't unusual on our street for one household to own multiple properties. One family in particular owned several of the houses on the block. The patriarch had wisely purchased multiple houses on our street all at once for all of the women in his family back when this old neighbourhood was considered affordable. When we had block parties, the small talk always started with, "Guess what so-and-so listed their house for," and "Guess how much we paid," and we would all pat ourselves on the back over our good fortune to buy right when we had (as though it wasn't just dumb luck). Our neighbour didn't like our half-blind dog, Lucy, who growled and barked whenever she walked by in her squeaky sneakers. This woman seemed exhausted by my presence at all times, and although I get along with most everyone, for some reason it was absolute dislike-at-first-sight from my side too. Like two hens pecking at each other, I puffed up my chest whenever she came by and stared down at her suspiciously. But there was nothing that she had actually done to warrant my dislike, other than not care for her home, which could have been for myriad reasons. Truthfully, I was never entirely sure why I was so irritated by her. It's not a feeling I have had often about people, instant wariness or distrust. Now I see that it was perhaps innate, and a trained response of internalized misogyny. I presumed it was perhaps, on some deep subconscious Freudian level, that her presence forced me to address the reality that I had moved on from my role as youthful and innocent maiden now that I was pregnant. I had officially shifted into the role of Mother; one step closer to Crone or Hag status, which was invariably "The End."

In Victoria Smith's book *Hags: The Demonisation of Middle-Aged Women*, she writes, "The cliché of middle-aged woman-hood is that it's a time when we 'become invisible.' Alas, superpower fans, this does not happen. We are still here, same as always; it's just that we are being ignored." I suspect I was already feeling tucked away and tolerated as a "fragile" pregnant woman, the last thing I wanted was to be ignored as a human being as well, and I wouldn't want to complain about it. "The implication is that any irritation we might now feel amounts to a hypocritical resentment at no longer being treated as sex objects," Smith goes on to say in *Hags*.

The first Crone archetype I came across in film was Meg Mucklebones from the 1985 movie *Legend* (which also starred a young Tom Cruise, and a buff and enormously horny Tim Curry as a Devil figure known as The Lord of Darkness, or just Darkness). Meg was a river hag who lurked below the surface like an alligator, pulling people underwater before devouring them, an aquatic cannibal. Her heavily water-logged flesh loosely covered her overly long torso, showing off rib bones like six-pack abs. Her green skin was phospho-rescent with algae. Any fat she had on her had navigated to odd places, like her shoulders and middle-back. Elephantine elf ears framed her witch face, which was as wrinkled as a shar-pei's, and her long, hooked nose dripped constantly. Her thin, kelp-like hair was worn in a comb-over on top of her head, hanging long down her back. It also covered her arms. When Tom Cruise's character crossed her path, Mucklebones greeted him flirtatiously saying, "What a fine, fat boy you are, Jack," and he in return fed her vanity and loneliness to fuel his escape by tricking her into thinking he was attracted to her. After a few cackles, Ms. Mucklebones told Jack she would make him happy by giving him one kiss before dying, but instead he sliced her head off with his broadsword. He did this because, as was confirmed in *The Shining*, old, saggy women who climb out of the water, whether it be a bathtub or a swamp, are bad news. So many cultures have a version of this character — call her Jenny Greenteeth in the UK, River Mumma in Jamaica, rusalka in Slavic cultures. She is

Yamauba in Kabuki theatre, and of course the Russians have Baba Yaga, who lived in a house with chicken legs for stilts that could walk around the woods.

Meg Mucklebones was terrifying to me as a child, but surprisingly, it wasn't the cannibalism that was disturbing. I'd read "Hansel and Gretel" and knew that old women who lived alone in the woods ate people. It was the body horror of her naturally aging, exposed breasts and flat ass. Female nudity was supposed to be artistic and beautiful, or sexy and pornographic, never hideous.

Our minds are hardwired to believe that the aging body has moved to a place beyond beauty and sexuality, to Meg's bog of revulsion. There was a theory posited in 1997 by the Rozin School that the reason for our negative reaction to the aging woman is existential anxiety. We instantaneously project ourselves into old bodies and are forced to briefly consider the inevitable endgame that we will all face one day. Aging women = death. Particularly an aging woman who has rejected the role of unpaid caregiver to others.

That's why the Crone is so often a fixture in horror, enough so to earn their own genre of "Hagsploitation" or "Psycho-Biddy" films from the 1960s through to the 1980s, including *What Ever Happened to Baby Jane?*, *Hush . . . Hush, Sweet Charlotte*, *Strait-Jacket*, and *Mommie Dearest*. Often these were the only meaty roles available for Oscar-winning leading ladies who had aged out of the system, like Bette Davis, Joan Crawford, and Faye Dunaway. As Jessica Lange says as Joan Crawford in Ryan Murphy's limited television series *Feud*, "Everything written for women seems to fall into just three categories: ingenues, mothers, or gorgons."

These films were created with misogyny in mind. Written by men, produced by men, they were the sweaty underside of the male gaze, designed for us to despise and find revulsion in the haggard faces, drooping bodies, and deranged behaviours of middle-aged, menopausal women who were not a dutiful housewife and mother. But something happened to subvert those characters in queer culture; they were put under the gay male gaze instead and came out looking fantastic. The Hags in these films may have chopped up their family members with axes or run them down with their cars, but queer audiences in particular adored their strength, proving you can smear a diva's makeup, but her glamour will still shine through her lipstick-stained teeth. In her autobiography, *The Lonely Life*, Bette Davis described her own birth as happening "between a clap of thunder and a streak of lightning. It almost hit the house and destroyed a tree out front."

Before facial fillers, botox, and even facelifts, Bette Davis's naturally aging, heavily painted face and sausage curls in *Whatever Happened to Baby Jane?* was the hook. Her appearance was what was most terrifying about the film, the grotesqueness of youth affixed to the aging body. To put it in modern perspective: Bette Davis was fifty-four when *Baby Jane* was released; Jennifer Lopez will be fifty-four at the time of this publication. But it was the banality about it all that defined the low-camp of Bette Davis's eyes doing backflips as she rolled them so hard at her nemesis Joan Crawford's put-upon wincing, as if the subtitle to the film could be "Suck It Up, Buttercup." We love the audaciousness of Baby Jane's absolute determination to continue to marinate in her youthful, awkward style for decades, an audaciousness which is only topped by her blatantly nefarious agenda. She hides nothing. Bette continued to play the terrifying crone well into her seventies in *The Watcher in the Woods*, a 1980 Disney live action foray into sci-fi/horror. Perhaps one of the first Disney movies with a trigger warning, "This is *not* a fairy tale," the title cards urged parents to pre-screen for their teenagers, as it was not suitable for small children.

None of the leading ladies in these movies were ideal mothers — barren physically or emotionally — and any children in the Hag's life were wrapped up in the violence of the storyline. Sadly, the real-life children of both Joan Crawford and Bette Davis also came out with tell-all books about addiction, and the psychological and physical abuse they endured at the hands of their mothers.

Crones and babies should not mix. The Crone doesn't just dislike babies, she consumes them. She draws children to her, only to cook them for dinner, like the Gingerbread Hag does with Hansel and Gretel. I'm sure that the Hag folklore in particular was designed to protect children from the dangers of wandering too near the water or too far into the forest alone. Hundreds of years ago, moms couldn't helicopter parent, they were too busy churning butter. Many children surely must have gotten lost or drowned in swamps and eaten by wild animals. But the message was really more damaging for women, not children. It was a warning: "Look what happens to women who reject traditional gender roles and motherhood!" Because women are meant to be working at building and sustaining families, not houses or careers or personal interests.

"Where a woman finds herself at forty, fifty, sixty, is not a direct expression of her politics, desires, or inner self. It's the result of a series of twists and turns: the jobs, the relationships, the pregnancies, the sick relatives, the dishes, the dust. It's the result of chance, of compromise and of coercion," Victoria Smith writes in *Hags*. And that coercion starts not with the father but with the mother, reading the fairy tales that remind us that the barren woman, the woman who rejects connecting herself with a family, is horrifying.

Eventually, we called pest control to come and take a look at the intruder living in our walls. I did my makeup and fixed my hair and sat up, swollen belly on display, happy for literally any company, even an exterminator. We chatted briefly before he got down on his knees next to the bed listening at the walls, knocking on the drywall, opening up a vent and shining a flashlight inside. He went outside the house, pulled out a ladder, and got up on the roof, waving at me from the outside. He came back in and stood with my then-wife by the bed.

"Well," he said, "you two got somethin' in common. You're both pregnant. It's a raccoon. She hasn't had the babies yet, so it'll either be any day now, or it could be a second litter in a few weeks. Sometimes they lose their first litter and have one later on in early summer. The kits will need a few weeks with her in there before they can see and hear. You'll hear lotsa chatter. What we'll do is, ah, put a door in over there by the entrance she ripped open, where she pulled the roof line up over there. She'll bring her little babies out to teach them how to get food and climb around. While they are out, we'll come back and put a latch on the door so they can't get back in. Evict 'em. They'll find someplace else to live," he finished.

While I was busy picturing an Alice in Wonderland–sized miniature door contraption for baby raccoons, my then-wife asked him if there was perhaps a faster way to do this, less humane maybe, but more . . . *permanent*, she intimated. He asked if she meant poachers, and I remember her being happy that he understood and wasn't being judgmental about it.

She explained, "I heard there are guys who have licences to deal with this situation. Otherwise, they just find a way to get back into your house. Chewing on the wiring. Ripping up the ducts. Pissing in the walls. They carry diseases, too, right? It's not going to be safe with a baby around." The exterminator told her that yes it was legal to do but regulated. It would cost around $250, and he knew a guy who knew a guy and could hook her up. Then he left us with a hefty $1,500 estimate for humane animal removal services and placed his card on the dresser on the way out. I remember thinking that it seemed completely backwards that doing the kind thing is always inevitably the more expensive route.

The minute he left I burst into tears. "YOU ARE NOT KILLING HER!" I yelled. "WE ARE PREGNANT! SHE IS A SINGLE MOTHER! SHE IS MY FRIEND!" I was near hysterics in my distress over the thought of it. My ex laughed and sat beside me, stroking my face. She used my nickname to calm me down, whispering, "Okay, Boots. Okay. Shh, now. No one is killing your pregnant friend. We'll let her have her babies. Shh, Boots. Shh." And under her breath she muttered, "Your pregnant friend is going to cost us fifteen hundred bucks."

Later, I considered if I had moved into my Little Edie years, the younger daughter of socialite Big Edie Bouvier Beale of *Grey Gardens* fame, a couple of hags who lived in squalor amongst vermin. She used to feed the raccoons who came in through the holes in their roof.

Listening to the chattering in the wall next to me, I would think about my furry friend and picture her building her little nest amongst the insulation. She was another mom, doing renovations on the same house. I remember reading somewhere that raccoons are brilliant mothers, on the list right under elephants, chimpanzees, polar bears, and pigs. They don't abandon their little ones. They teach them how to hunt and trap food, how to open a garbage bin lid. They teach them how to avoid predators like dogs and the odd coyote that still roams city streets. They create a warm, soft home for their babies and care for them for months. But even when you are a great mother, when it becomes inconvenient financially, mothers are often put out and find the door has been locked behind them.

I wanted to be a good mom to our baby too. I related to this much-maligned trash panda. It was entertainment for me watching her try to squeeze her big belly out of the small hole she had pried open along the side of our porch roof. She seemed awfully busy for a heavily pregnant ball of fur. I was sometimes a little jealous of her freedom and ability to nest. She could just roll her furry pregnant self out to bring back one of those half-wet, balled up T-shirts left on the street, or a single gutter sock, lay it over some insulation, and make a cozy little bed for her kits. I couldn't even leave my room to pick out a crib. These little materialistic joys of being pregnant were lost to me, and I was mostly okay with that, but something about my outburst made me realize how lonely I was in this experience of building our life. My ex had her friends, and she had plumbers and electricians to deal with, which, although stressful, was still people. She had a job to go to. Multiple purposes. I had one: gestate.

In some ways, pregnancy made me feel very animalistic and primal. In other ways, I felt alien and supernatural, lying here in my pod, building a spinal column and mapping out neural pathways for another human to join the planet. But I didn't feel productive. With the construction, I could see the house coming together. Where there was no kitchen, now there was a kitchen. When a wall went up, you knew it. It was loud. Conspicuous. Everything I was doing was the size of a poppyseed if it was even visible to the human eye at all. I mean, I was sitting up here in bed dividing neural progenitor cells into neurons and glia and forming the basis of the central nervous system of *our child*, and all I got for doing that was heartburn.

Sometimes, I felt like the only way to get any peace from it all was to disconnect from this body of mine and retreat into my mind. Stare out the window and watch the next surprising being that would end up on the roof — whether it be an unwed mother raccoon, or a chance to spy on my next-door neighbour. I was willing to be more generous in my spirit, and feel more connected and relate to a pregnant raccoon, than I was to the lady next door because of internalized misogyny. I was more committed to propping up this patriarchal gaslighting, and our home equity, than I was to seeing her for who she really was.

The older I get the more I think about my neighbour. Apparently, she was either a mathematician or a scientist, possibly a rocket scientist, something light years away from a theatre major like me. She and I spoke very different languages when it came to describing the world. I could acknowledge that there were many very impressive qualities in this woman. She wasn't afraid of anything or anyone. She seemed to be able to figure out anything — electrical, plumbing, roofing — all on her own. She was completely independent financially. For a single woman her age to have achieved so much independence, to the point where she could afford five houses, was astonishing, really. I assumed I would be tied to one crippling mortgage well into my sixties. Instead, I lost my home like the raccoons, years later, in the divorce.

Maybe becoming a Crone wasn't the most frightening future. At that time, I was afraid of everything. Unexplained noises in my own home. My own body. I was vulnerable, hiding away and dependent on others to bring me food, and I was trying hard not to be angry or bitter about my situation, but that was becoming increasingly untenable. I was projecting my own anger on an aged woman, past her most fertile years, who was sticking out her proudly hairy chin and doing whatever the fuck she wanted without waiting for permission or an expert to tell her how to proceed. She wasn't like young women, trussed and tied up tight, and packaged like meat under plastic wrap.

In fact, as I age, I start to envy old Meg Mucklebones's feminist utopia. Like a lot of mature women, I fantasize often about moving into a cabin in the woods as far away from responsibilities as I can get. Childfree, connected to nature, out by a river, wandering around her property, brazen in her nudity in a way only women over forty can be. No laundry, with her days free to pursue her hobbies and nights for potential passion with a young Tom Cruise. It sounds like a dream.

THE BITCH

(OR, SHE'S THE BOSS)

"I'm not bossy. I'm the boss."

— BEYONCÉ

Some horror movies leave traces that linger in the recesses of your mind only to jump out and scare you years later. Every long hotel hallway I walk down has *The Shining* twins at the end of it. And every unfinished basement inevitably has a corner occupied by a grown man standing facing the wall; a gift from watching *The Blair Witch Project* back in 1999 with a co-worker shortly before the end of my short-lived career in large scale musical theatre. The marketing build-up around *The Blair Witch Project* had been overpowering — people everywhere were raving about this low-budget indie horror flick that was changing the zeitgeist. A little movie made up of spliced together pieces of discarded footage, with no script and no named actors, was becoming a phenomenon, earning over $200 million in profit and disrupting entertainment marketing. The filmmakers, a group of four guys who came from an advertising background making commercials, were hailed as new industry leaders not only in genre but in marketing and tech, as they helped develop the way we all learned to use digital marketing to connect with fan bases. These filmmakers started by breaking a sacred covenant — they lied about the movie and said it was a true story when it wasn't, and then they asked the public to write their honest opinion about the possibility that they might be lying on public forums to provoke discourse. They continued the bold-faced lies in interviews, on television, in magazines, and on web bulletin boards and internet forums, pulling all of us into a Mandela effect where many people felt they had heard the urban legend before. They built fake websites to corroborate their story, generated fake news articles. They devised an entire fictional digital universe around their low-budget movie. They even claimed to have been contacted by the parents of the deceased filmmakers in the documentary.

I wasn't really frightened by it when I first saw it, though — I was actually utterly irritated. It was the opposite of what I was aligned with at the company I was working for, a slick mega-musical theatrical organization with high production values and artistic integrity. This film was unpolished, nauseatingly jarring, with rough and disjointed audio, imperceptible but for one voice — that of the director, a character named Heather Donahue. Her grating, nagging, critical, passive-aggressive voice, bitching at her two male crew members through the whole movie, came through loud and clear. This film and that character ran counter to my sanctimony as a twenty-five-year-old musical theatre purist who loved the classics but wanted to develop new voices and new talents. I wanted to lead in my own style, feminine, but, you know, without being a bitch.

It wasn't a happy workplace, although the work we did was exciting. Getting to work alongside glittering Broadway celebrities and creative geniuses was thrilling and disenchanting all at once. A little like visiting actual Broadway. One day I might be watching Ann Reinking teach a room full of dancers about the intricacies of a Fosse bent wrist. Another day I could sit with Joel Grey while he chirped like a proud pappa about his daughter, Jennifer. Once, I started to usher a man out of our rehearsal room who was asking to play the piano only to realize it was Marvin Hamlisch. I had a Donny Osmond purple disco jumpsuit–clad doll as a child, and now Donny himself was walking past me in the production office. It was magic. All of it.

But I was also often afraid. The workplace was extremely volatile and full of future #MeToo stories. As a young, inexperienced, overly naive woman I was in way over my head. I was scared of mid-level managers who would launch into vicious tirades and temper tantrums over what seemed like small things. I was scared to pick up the telephone, never knowing which agent, actor, or member of the creative team would be hollering at me. There was a thick layer of tension over every conversation. I was terrified most of all of the sixth floor, the Executive Suite, and the screams that came down from it through the air ducts and elevator shaft from the big boss's office. There was no HR department back then. There was no route to find support. Any complaint was met with, "Do you know how many thousands of young women would want your job?"

In the faux documentary, the Blair Witch Project is an idea of Heather's. She's a film student directing a documentary about the urban legend of the Blair Witch with the goal of paying respect to a "true crime" story, a not-so-urban (more Southern Gothic) legend that she has been obsessed with in a pre-true-crime-fanatic era. Heather wants everyone to know how book smart she is and shows the audience her credentials by way of a stack of research tomes she proudly displays at the beginning of the film. A survival book, a historical work describing the legends, and a detailed map of the area.

I knew the Heather-type. I went to school with Heather-types. That young woman at the front of the class with her hand perpetually raised, the Reese-Witherspoon-in-*Election* look-alike who had her essays done a week in advance, who ironed her shirts instead of picking them up off the floor and tossing them in the dryer for ten minutes. The young woman who insisted on being the lead on every group project and then complained that none of the rest of us were pulling our weight. Young women like me who were sliding into class just after the bell rang, slipping a week-overdue essay on the bottom of the pile on the prof's desk, called this kind of person *bossy*, but what we really meant was *bitchy*. And I suppose the kind of scorn that I probably indirectly dished out onto the Heathers of my school was similar to what I received in my first job from the women at my office, a righteous helping of "who the hell does she think she is sashaying in here?" My youthful entitle-ment was seen as disrespectful to their hard labour and years spent working their way up. They were the gatekeepers to the glass ceiling, and I swanned in, bathing in the sunlight, expect-ing it to be my skylight. As for me, I looked at the girls like Heather and put them down because I was jealous that they were disciplined in the areas I was not. I was jealous that they claimed leadership while I played a supporting role. I wanted to lead, I had the creativity, but I didn't have the spreadsheets leading required.

In the film, Heather manages a crew of two. A long-haired cameraman named Josh, who arrives late, likely thanks to an intense game of Hacky Sack in the quad, and Michael, a friend-of-a-friend who is handling the audio because, well, it's a gig. Heather is the one in charge. She is the holder of the map and the keeper of the Hi8 camcorder. She has organized all their equipment and plotted out the entire two-day trip. Her plan is to chat with a few locals, get some B-roll, and then head up to the woods to see where the supernatural occurrences went down. Despite dire warnings from locals, Heather's plan (and hubris) has her determined to lead her intrepid crew to the two major sites involved in the myth: Coffin Rock, the site of a massacre, and a cemetery where the witch is meant to be buried.

The Blair Witch is actually a two-part legend. The first part goes back to the eighteenth century when a woman named Elly Kedward was tried and convicted of being a witch and was banished to live in the woods as punishment. That's the gist and totality of that story, a mythology with all the trimmings: supernatural dark forces, a creepy forest, and a vengeful woman.

The second part of the legend took place in the 1940s when seven children in the township of Blair went missing. It was later discovered that a hermit had built a house in the woods where he would bring the kidnapped children. Rustin Parr would take these kids to the basement in pairs and leave one standing in the corner while he murdered the second. When Rustin was finally caught, he blamed Elly Kedward for his behaviour, saying the spirit of the two-hundred-year-old witch had possessed him. Which of course, in 1940, sounded more likely than believing a psychopathic pedophile might murder multiple children. So, the town renamed itself Burkittsville to escape its bad reputation, and, since the end of the child murders, everyone in town managed to avoid going into the woods.

Watching Heather jump through hoops to find a leadership style the men would respect was exhausting. First, she tried to be a "cool girl," hanging with the boys by teasing them and smoking cigarettes. She even made fart jokes. At the hotel she drank Scotch, only to make faces and then admit that she "hates Scotch." She clearly didn't enjoy any of these male-oriented activities, so everything she tried was an inauthentic misfire. A "pick-me" girl before we had words for that. Being friendly with them didn't seem to make them pick up the camera when they needed to, or record the audio. In fact, a huge part of her job scope as leader seemed to include reminding them multiple times over that she is, in fact, a competent leader.

In a night scene beside the campfire, Heather compares their situation to *Gilligan's Island* — "Yeah but this ship has a good captain, not a fat beer-guzzling captain" — only to be quickly reminded by the men that not only is there no beer on the island, but they'd called their "leader" the Skipper. Heather can't even relate to the reasons the boys tease; she has to ask them why they're laughing at her when her feet get wet. She doesn't speak their language. They might be in the forest, but the proverbial mental treehouse the boys occupy has a sign that says *no girlz allowed*.

There are rules to society and the gendered world we inhabit, or so we are led to believe — natural laws that must be obeyed or expect consequences. Heather is a woman trying to lead two men through a traditionally masculine domain to create a form of work in a field that has statistically been male dominated — documentary. No matter how brave Heather is, she is working with a broken compass, and so they are doomed to go in circles. She's a bitch in the woods hunting down a witch, a symbol of feminine power. Witches have to be punished, and so do bitches.

For me, after first working as an unpaid intern for fourteen hours a day, six days a week for months on end, I was offered a full-time job, and then one to two years later was offered a lateral promotion. It didn't offer any more money, but it was in the department I wanted to be in, where the action was, so to speak. I was both excited and scared — excited about the opportunity and nervous about what taking it entailed. It would mean working on the executive floor and being surrounded by conflict and dodging uncomfortable situations at all times.

But it turns out I didn't need to worry, because my boss, one of the only female senior executives on the team, blocked the job offer and took the decision out of my hands. She pulled me into her corner office, shut the door, and gently broke the news to me that I was not going to be moving up. I couldn't understand why she had sabotaged me (which was how I saw it at the time). She had been incredibly supportive, kind, and helpful as a boss so far. A calm and elegant centre amongst the toxic chaos. When I asked her why, she explained that part of my education in business was in understanding that she wasn't there to be my mother or teacher. She was looking out for her whole team while trying to survive, and in this very toxic workplace full of political maneuvering, she was trying to assert her own leadership. They should have asked her first before offering me the job, they should have considered the implications of losing headcount in her department. For the white women of the '80s and '90s, breaking that glass ceiling meant some people below might get cut by falling shards.

At the time, I was a "gee golly, let's put on a show" style theatre nerd. I thought making art was collaborative, I thought women were there to lift each other up, and I didn't understand how a woman could block another woman's success in a male-dominated field. Why would women ever work against each other?

But years later, I recognized that she was also protecting me. The executive floor was a dangerous place, and I was an exceedingly naive young woman. Bright but anxious, trusting, and not at all strategic. I would have been eaten alive. She wasn't my mother, but she did what my mother would have wanted her to do — she kept me safe. She wasn't my teacher, but I sure learned a few things.

In 2015, a study in the *Journal of Personality and Social Psychology* posited that there are twelve characteristics of heroism: bravery, conviction, courage, determination, helpfulness, honesty, inspirational, protective, self-sacrificing, selflessness, strength, and moral integrity. There are no "heroes" in *The Blair Witch Project*, although you can see that Heather was trying. True heroes are a rarity — that's why they are so special — and yet we demand heroics of our leaders, despite the circumstances they face. It's an impossible task for anyone to lead and maintain hero status, so it's no wonder why people shy away from stepping to the front. Heroes get attacked, it's in the job description. Furthermore, not many of those characteristics are typically aligned with socially constructed, gendered ideas about women in power, and so women are already at a disadvantage.

Studies have shown that the longer a woman has been in the workforce, the less likely she is to want a female boss. A 2011 study out of UCLA reported that the majority of female participants preferred male leadership over other females, and referred to women leaders with words like *emotional*, *catty*, and *bitchy*. In the world of law, it was worse, with only three percent of participants saying they would work for a female associate. Yale student Robin Ely took the study one step further by positing that women "respond to the situation they're in." Going back to the legal world, Ely surveyed people at male-dominated law firms and then contrasted those surveys with people at firms where the leadership was more mixed. In the male-dominated firms, women were "almost universally reviled," and provided little support to each other. Of course, this had a stronger impact on women of colour, as they had to manage both race- and gender-based discrimination. This was not the case in more gender-balanced workplaces.

In *The Blair Witch Project*, Heather cycles through every tactic she can find to try to gain the respect of the men before finally turning to the traditionally supportive mother role, which is when they finally accept her. She goes so far as to sew one of the men's pants during a dark, scary night in their shared tent while surrounded by disembodied screams. I learned while editing this book that the actress reportedly regularly mended her co-star's pants as part of her work on the set.

When Heather turns the camera on herself at the beginning of the film, she is picture perfect, posed, and almost insufferably intellectual — a confident portrait of a leader. But in the iconic, snotty close-up selfie scene at the end of the film, we find her psychologically broken, spiritually lost, without hope, and calling out for her mother.

For those who grew up with mothers it is fairly inevitable that when we are at the end of our rope, or in trauma, we call out for them. Mothers are supposed to be our first leader in life, our one-person cheering squad, the one who is supposed to give their life for our protection Perhaps that is why the first thing Heather does in her farewell video is apologize to all of their mothers. Heather accepts a hundred percent of the blame for their position, saying that all of the horror they are experiencing is her fault as a poor leader, and she lists her two moral failings: she was naive and she insisted on everything. She emphasizes that word over and over — she *insisted* on things being *her way* — and now they are hungry, cold, and hunted. Because she insisted.

I left musical theatre shortly after *The Blair Witch Project* came out. The magic was gone. The leaders of the company I worked for were arrested and found guilty of fraud and forgery, and the company was shuttered. It turned out the men on the sixth floor were showmen who were creating illusions in the accounting books as well as on stage. The judge in the case said, "The exponential growth of the company was analogous to an athlete taking a performance-enhancing drug. The result may be spectacular, but the means involve cheating." During the trial, the judge said that all of the company's successes "were built upon a platform of falsehoods and manipulation." While we were down on the lower floors dreaming up amazing shows, these captains of industry were standing around their financial statements, like witches over a cauldron, cooking the books. My immediate boss was not implicated — it turns out that she was not the bad guy but the moral compass that I should have been steering myself by.

More women in senior leadership is unquestionably the best way forward. As *Harvard Business Review* recently advised future leaders: "Don't command; empathize . . . Twenty-first century leadership demands that leaders establish an emotional connection with their followers . . . Men can learn a lot about how to do this effectively by watching and emulating women."

At the end of *The Blair Witch Project*, Heather and Mike are supernaturally drawn to an abandoned house in the woods by the screams of their lost friend. Mike drops his camera, but Heather keeps a hold on hers until it seems ripped out of her cold, dead hand after the final terrifying shot of Mike standing in the corner, leaving me to wonder if maybe the real killer wasn't the witch at all — maybe it was the spirit of serial killer Rustin Parr trying to keep his legend alive, not quite finished after all. Maybe *he* was the real culprit, and the Blair Witch was just another powerful woman taking the fall for a man's abusive actions. Maybe we have the whole thing backwards.

THE MAN AT THE END OF THE BED

(TERRIFYING TALES FROM BEYOND THE BALCONY)

"The side of fairy tales I don't like is that
they always have happy endings, that there
is just good and evil, and things are perfect.
But life is a little more complicated."

— ANGELINA JOLIE

T he thing about castles is they're so aspirational. You imagine
it would be lovely to live in one, but you don't really think
about the cost of heating them or how long they would take to
vacuum. Keeping any basement dry is hard enough without a
moat to consider. Still, castles seem fantastic. I can't remember
a single story I read as a young child that didn't end with the
domestically abused girl making a strategic move into a castle as
she entered womanhood. Or a misfit gang of elves and dwarves
storming one. A castle is fairy tale goals. Except for the towers,
which are to be avoided. Towers have no entrances or exits, they
have pointy needles that put you to sleep and captive weavers
with long names and a penchant for riddles.

For a time, when I was in my early twenties, two girlfriends
and I rented a little house that sat in the shadow of a castle. I
had the primary bedroom, a room that in any episode of *House*

Hunters would have been described as "spacious" and "full of character." My bed butted up against a wall of exposed red brick next to the best feature of all: a Juliet balcony. It looked out on Casa Loma, which was really more a mansion, a pretend castle that has been a location for countless movies and television shows shot in Toronto (actual castles being in short supply in North America).

I loved my Juliet balcony. I put a little folding chair out there, and at night I would sit and contemplate my future and my love life, as Juliet herself likely did on hers. Unlike Juliet, I smoked menthol cigarettes on mine because a glamorous blonde friend had called them a breath of fresh air. Our street was dimly lit with wonderful large trees that cast complex, occasionally ominous, shadows. In the garden out back, someone had long ago planted exotic herbs and vegetables like rhubarb and greens that seemed far out of my capabilities to ever actually prepare. It all felt incredibly romantic — this house, this balcony, this castle, this life.

Attached to our house was an almost identical little house, but in that house lived three boys. One was loud, tall, and gangly with a mop of black hair, whom I will call Paul. The second boy was quiet, short, blonde, and reminded me of the boy who gave me my first sloppy, teeth-smacking kiss. I will call him Jason. The third wore glasses, was prematurely balding, and was clearly the leader of the group. I will call him Mark. Mark was an inciter of entertainment and an argumentative drunk. Nights with Mark usually ended with him in a scuffle.

As young women, we were excited with the prospect of having a house of our own, and we painted, primped, and nested like starlings. As young men, they were intoxicated both by the freedom of adulthood and by the cases of cheap beer they poured down their gullets. Every night around 8 p.m. it began — pulsing bass beats from their stereo — and it would continue until one of us went over in abject frustration to complain or threaten to call the cops. I often wondered if these repetitive drum solos were an invitation to party or a summons to war. The two households were not alike in dignity.

The boys had lived on the street longer than we had. Paul had a story about almost every house, which he whispered in menacing tones. "See that one with the boarded-up windows? The father kept his daughter and her baby locked in the basement for years until one day she escaped, chopped her father into pieces, and burned the house to the ground." I pointed out the flaws in his narrative by reminding him that the house was still standing. Having three brothers myself, I was used to boys trying to get a rise out of me. Many of my memories as a young child are of slamming bedroom doors and white-hot tears of frustration when one of my brothers had dismembered my Wonder Woman doll as if to say, "Not so immortal now, are you Diana?" But the limbs would be snapped back on again by my mother and my outrage placated with phrases like "all back in one piece" and "no harm done." These were the tiny terrors imagined by little boys to get little girls to . . . what? Sometimes I wondered if it was to test my loyalty; would I rat them out? Or could it have been jealousy? Did they want to play with those toys? I know I coveted their Stretch Armstrong and twenty-sided colourful dice. "They are trying to get your attention; don't give it to them," my mother would say. I would ignore them, and they would up the stakes, until they aged out of tormenting their younger sister and moved on to dating her friends instead. Adulthood meant having to take these battles on myself, without a referee.

Occasionally, when she was performing in a show, our landlord would come and stay in the basement apartment of our little house. She was the first professional opera singer I had ever met. She had long straight brown hair and round, wide-set Shelley Duvall eyes. She came from a small and friendly town, which became very apparent one morning when she hustled upstairs with exuberance. "Girls! I have wonderful news," she said. "We are going to have our windows cleaned for free!" Now granted, this was not even on the charts of what we would consider wonderful news, but we loved her, so we feigned excitement.

"A young man was banging and banging on the front door at three in the morning. He said his car had broken down and he heard that there were three nice girls who lived here who would help him. He said in exchange for using our phone and some money to get the car towed he would come back today and wash the windows!" she said, ecstatically happy.

I think it was at about this point that one of us, jaw dropped with astonishment, posed the question: "You let him in?"

"Of course I did," she said. "He was stranded! I got him fifty dollars and off he went," her already preternaturally wide eyes were getting wider and wider as she noted our skepticism. "Do you think it was a scam?" she finally asked.

A stranger had been allowed into our house while we slept. But we didn't call the police. Nothing had happened. A man had knocked on the door, she let him in, she gave him money, he left. We all felt wise and cosmopolitan in comparison to her simple, country ways. Who would let a stranger in at 3 a.m.? And who was this person who knew *three nice girls* lived here? Was he going to come back?

Of course, our mystery man didn't show that day, or the next. Our views of the city from indoors stayed streaked and clouded with condensation. I made hearts in the fog with my fingers and wrote my lover's name in them.

So, we three nice girls who lived in the house by the castle kept living. We worked during the days while the older men at work watched us, and we danced in the evenings in tight circles around our purses while the young men at clubs watched us. And in our quiet time, we curled up on the couch eating ice cream by the bowlful and tried to figure out who dismembered the women on episodes of *Law and Order*.

I slept like the dead on weekends, the way only a young woman with no one who depended on her can. The room was quiet, dark, and mine. Night turned to dawn, which turned to morning, and morning sometimes turned to noon before I woke. I could be oblivious to it all there, even the passing of time.

I was even oblivious to the eyes that were on me while I lay slumbering in my queen-size bed by the castle.

It was around three o'clock in the morning. A man whispered my name. That must have been what woke me. I don't remember exactly. I only remember that I was sleeping and then I wasn't. My name was a whisper in the mouth of a stranger. I have never had much in the way of senses. I have almost no sense of smell, and without my contact lenses everyone is a blurry form with a bit of colour. I saw a shape at the end of my bed. Short. Stocky. I heard it whispering my name, over and over, like he had a very important secret to share with me. I didn't say anything. I'm not even sure if I exhaled after I gasped. The shape whispered, "I want to cuddle."

I recognized the voice. It wasn't a stranger. It was the boy next door. Silent Jason. He had drunkenly toddled into my bedroom like a sleepwalking child. I was instantly reassured because it was a cuddle he asked for. He didn't want to pull my arms off and leave me in a ditch. I was safe. Right? But wasn't that what Sidney Prescott thought when Billy Loomis crawled through her window in *Scream* for a PG-13 cuddle-fest?

A jumble of words tumbled out of me quickly — "No, Jason. It's late, Jason. I have to work tomorrow, Jason" — but he was immovable. He had planted himself stubbornly at the end of my bed and said again, more insistently this time, "I want to cuddle." Suddenly, it didn't seem innocent. And it didn't seem like a request anymore. Perhaps to distract him, I asked him how he had gotten into my room, and he pointed to my balcony. I wondered if this was how thirteen-year-old Juliet had felt at first when her much older Romeo bypassed the security features and appeared outside her bedroom. These violent delights have violent ends. My balcony no longer felt romantic.

There is a frequently referenced movie trope known as the Beast in the Boudoir, usually depicted by a vampire slipping into a woman's bedroom through a window, sliding across the floor, and bending over her sleeping form. I will admit to have fallen for the implied sexiness of this platitude. A gentleman serenades a woman outside her window, a beast climbs in through it. The first poem I ever wrote as a tween romanticized the idea of a vampire visiting me in my dreams. In real life, though, it wasn't the sensation I expected. In dreams, I consented to the visitation. Here, I had not because I was unconscious.

I still had my voice, but my body was frozen in fear. I didn't leave my bed, and he didn't move either. It was a stalemate, the blankets a wall between us. I feared if either of us moved the tension would shift, and something would have had to be done about that. I wanted to run, but my body wouldn't move, so I tried to calm both myself and him. I remember using the only thing I had in my arsenal, my words. I was louder and more forceful: "Go home, Jason. You are scaring me." And to my shock and utter relief, he did.

I still don't want to think he meant me any harm. I am not sure he, in his drunken stupor, realized how frightening it would be for me to be woken by a man standing at the end of my bed. Frankly, now that I am past forty, I can't be bothered to judge what his inebriated, entitled thought process was anymore. I am just glad he went back out my balcony door the same way he came in, climbed over onto his own balcony, and slunk back inside. Once I was sure he was gone, I jumped up, pushed a small dresser in front of the door, and crawled back into my bed. I didn't call the police because I knew him. And what was I going to do? Have him arrested? Ruin his life for wanting to cuddle? That's how it would be seen. Nothing happened. Just a little drunk mischief. If he had been a stranger, the situation would have been very different.

Google *man at the end of my bed*, and you'll find 2,330,000,000 results. It's everyone's nightmare. Because it happens. Even in Canada, twenty-three people out of every hundred thousand will experience a "home invasion." The term is a bit of an amalgamation of a few crimes, and I'll compress that complicated bit into one sentence: a burglary or unwelcome entrance into a person's home by someone known or unknown, when someone is known to be at home. Single women and senior citizens seem to be the predominant targets. The scenario that played out in my bedroom ended with me coming out physically safe but a little mentally shaky for a while. This is not the reality for a huge number of vulnerable people who were accosted in their most vulnerable state — unconscious — in the place where they are supposed to be the safest — locked away in their home.

In the days afterwards, I felt embarrassed about what had happened. But embarrassment and powerlessness show up the same way in the body. Your belly button curves inwards and your shoulders hunch, you bow your head more, you tremble a little and feel sick. So it's easy to confuse the two. All of the same excuses that women have been using to protect men since the dawn of time, I used. And shortly thereafter, I decided it was time for me to leave the castle. I moved into a new apartment with my best friend. It was almost twice the cost of the house, but we liked our bunker-like basement apartment with three small windows (all with bars on them). When we weren't working, drinking, or dancing at clubs, our evenings were spent peering through the holes of our crocheted blankets at Diane Keaton learning her lessons in a well-played VHS copy of *Looking for Mr. Goodbar*, or at Alfred Hitchcock's *Psycho*.

I was in my twenties back then. Now I'm in my forties. I have aged a lot, I've built a fortress of protective flesh around me (by way of forty pounds that I don't seem interested enough to lose), and I wish I could tell you that was the only time someone broke into my home while I was alone and sleeping, but it wasn't. It happened to me again in May 2022. Someone broke into my home at 4 a.m. He was wearing a construction vest and carrying tools according to my neighbour, whose dog alerted him to the situation (my dog snored through it all). The man was standing in my backyard reading some papers, and my neighbour assumed he was a diligent gardener that I had hired to prune some trees before the crack of dawn on a Thursday. This faux gardener used the tools he carried to slice through a screen, open a main floor window, and come into my kitchen, spilling some things before leaving. He stole nothing, but he left behind an iPad with a cracked screen and a blank children's birthday card with a cat vomiting rainbows on the front of it, both items laid out neatly on the front seat of my car in my garage. His house or condo keys with a security fob attached and the papers he was reading were found in the bushes by my window where he had been hiding.

The first time someone broke into my house while I slept, I did not make use of my available privilege of calling the police. In the second experience, I wielded my white-middle-class entitlement and it failed me. The police did not follow up on the break-in attempt. They determined, without any proof, that it was a mentally ill, underhoused man, likely a bottle scavenger, who had thought he might try escalating to B and E, and not to worry. After bagging up the evidence and taking some photos, the police returned the evidence to me and said they wouldn't be needing it. As they recommended, I purchased multiple security cameras.

My break-in was on May 12, 2022. Two weeks later, on May 27, 2022, two blocks away from me, I read on our community's social media page that a man was found standing in a woman's backyard with his pants down, peeping in through her window. This was apparently the third time he had done this at that house. The homeowner saw him, ran outside, chased him down, and verbally confronted him. They argued, during which time the homeowner took a photo of the man and reported him to the police. The police told this neighbour that, yes, they were aware of this particular peeping Tom, that he had been a "long-time problem," and they suspected he had escalated to entering homes recently as well. Two streets over from my house. He was finally arrested a few days later after peeping in another woman's house — for the seventh or eighth time over several weeks. This woman's partner chased him down and held him until the police came and arrested him, but they told the woman that he likely would not be held for very long, if at all. I don't know that this is the same man, but it would have been wonderful if the police had checked some fingerprints or looked into it.

Not that voyeurism is necessarily transgressive or inherently violent. I wouldn't kink-shame. Many people enjoy *consensual* voyeurism as a healthy, fun part of their life or relationship. The urge to be voyeuristic is inherent in all of us. Film, literature, and art have trained us to look at the world through the "othering" white male gaze. When we are alone in our own homes, we watch reality TV of other people's homes, their home make-overs and house tours. We are desperate to see the inside world of others, which is probably why, as a crime, voyeurism isn't taken very seriously. From what I understand after a conversation with a criminal lawyer friend in my city, being in someone's backyard without permission, looking inside someone's window, hiding in trees, standing on the sidewalk and peering in, are actions frequently downgraded to mischief, and crimes that are rarely enforced. Especially if they have a "reason" for looking through the window.

From what I was told, courts start to take things seriously when property is involved or recordings are made. Intention is important; if you go into someone's yard with the intention to steal something or cause mischief, then it's called prowling at night. And when a person surreptitiously makes a *visual* recording of a person who is in circumstances that give rise to a reasonable expectation of privacy it's very illegal. Like when Jimmy Stewart and Grace Kelly in *Rear Window* looked through a camera's zoom lens into other peoples' apartments and took photos. That wasn't very princess-like behaviour for a member of a royal family.

Decades have passed since my castle-adjacent life, but nothing much has changed, it seems. Some men are still going door-to-door spreading fear. But I'm a very different person now. I'm a mother. I have daughters of my own who are edging towards freedom. I want them to make sure they never willingly invite violence into their home, and to also know that if it finds its way in anyways, it isn't their fault. I want to remind them that ultimately far more will be pardoned than punished, but they should still always fight for accountability. I want them to be vigilant, but not live in fear, to ensure that they put thought and planning and sometimes expense into maintaining their safety. Safety first.

But they don't want to hear about that from their old mom. That's the thing about youth — everything seems so fantastical. You envision yourself completely invincible from harm, and you don't really consider the cost of your safety. Everything seems so full of positive potential in the first years away from your parents' home.

I just want them to live happily ever after.

THE BABYSITTER

(CHANGING DIAPERS AND NARRATIVES)

"There's something incredibly seductive
about youth . . . I think it just has different
forms and it's how you survive it, and whether
you choose to be victimized by it. It's not in
my nature to be a victim."

— BROOKE SHIELDS

I don't remember how I got the job. Maybe it was through my best friend, Jane, or maybe she got the job from me. All I remember is that for the better part of a year, when I was in grade nine, both Jane and I would babysit regularly for a family that had moved into our suburban neighbourhood. This wasn't like any family I had met before. The mothers in our neighbourhood all shared a similar haircut that was likely the result of them going to the same Italian stylist, Gino. A remnant of the Princess Diana years, the cut was a slightly feathered, short-long pixie, dyed either a rusty, not-quite-strawberry blonde or a brownish-black, as though they couldn't quite decide on one colour. They wore Northern Reflections sweaters or cardigans with a simple button-down peeking out from beneath, light-washed Mom-jeans if they were casual moms and elastic-waisted polyester slacks if they were more formal. They wore simple jewellery, simple makeup, and simple shoes. Their entire look was designed to not attract attention. The focus was never on them, but on their role. The message their looks sent was that they were always available for hugs. You never worried about something sharp poking out of the fabric or catching on you, or it being so fragile it might tear. You didn't have to worry about ruining something expensive if you accidentally spilled something on them. These moms were Scotchgarded and durable. But that wasn't this woman, the mother we were babysitting for.

If I had to guess, I would say she was in her late thirties or early forties and had been a high-fashion model at some point, or, at the very least, she could have been because she seemed to tower above other women. I picture her as having stood over six feet, but that might have been a combination of her big hair and tall heels. She was blessed with an abundance of can't-possibly-ignore-them spiral curls. That hair. It was organized chaos. I had been forever trying to conceal or tame my own frizzy mess while she positively celebrated hers. Mine was auburn in a dull sense, whereas hers was a deep, committed black that conjured up thoughts of nightclubs and moonlight. Her skin was permanently tanned like she had spent weeks in the Mediterranean. Her makeup was always colourful, thickly rimmed black kohl around her gray eyes, her wide, white-toothed smile contrasting her orangey-red lipstick. She even cooked differently than other mothers. There was no macaroni and cheese here. It was Chicken Marbella or coq au vin on a Tuesday night.

And her clothes. Her clothes were extraordinary. They skirted past garish and right into chic, always tight against her incredibly slender body. She wore pencil-thin miniskirts and high stiletto heels, blouses with massive floral prints or jewelled epaulets, sequined cocktail dresses and long beaded evening gowns. She was not afraid to flaunt her femininity, a kind of femininity that I had always dreamed of but had yet to see modelled in real life.

This couple had moved here from another country, and even her elegant accent seemed theatrical and expensive. Her love for her children was just as ebullient as her clothing. The children were a pleasure to be with. As babysitting goes, it was a great gig. It was weekly, and they paid an enormous amount in comparison to what my friends were making. Instead of the usual five dollars an hour, max, this woman paid an astounding ten dollars an hour, and she had usually cooked a phenomenal dinner already. The house was tidy-ish. All I had to do was feed the children, play with them, give them a bath, and put them in bed by nine. And then I had three hours to myself with their incredible collection of VHS tapes.

The father had only one thing that interested me: an entire wall-to-wall bookshelf in his home office of films from around the world. Obscure titles I had never seen at our suburban Blockbuster. There was a slant to his film choices that led towards the sensual: *The Unbearable Lightness of Being*, *Henry & June*, *The Cook, the Thief, His Wife & Her Lover*, *Sex, Lies, and Videotape*, *9 ½ weeks*. Sensuality was the overall atmosphere of their home too. It was almost overpowering. Or maybe it was just my own burgeoning sexuality that made everything feel romantic and passionate in the world; I was The Babysitter after all.

There was a movie that flew in and out of theatres in the mid-'90s, pitched as an erotic thriller/horror called *The Babysitter*, starring Alicia Silverstone and featuring a fantastic soundtrack.

The trailer's logline was something like, "The husband had desires, the wife had suspicions. The boyfriend had ideas. Here's to a night of endless possibilities." With this film, Guy Ferland was graduating to director after being a personal assistant to Joel Schumacher. The screenplay was adapted by Robert Coover, based on his short story, in which the father's narrative flips seamlessly between the "real world" where the babysitter is a young, gentle and naive girl, to his violent and highly sexual inner world. And like Marilyn Monroe's character in *The Seven Year Itch*, a much tamer older sibling to *The Babysitter*, Silverstone's character isn't even given a name until the very end of the film, and she seems oblivious to the chaos she is causing in the pants of men everywhere. Everyone — in both the story and the film — is obsessed with the coquettish babysitter, including the ten-year-old boy who is her charge.

Two teenage boys from her school — her current boyfriend, a straight-A student, and her Iago-esque former boyfriend/sociopath — know she will be alone babysitting and spy on her while plotting to assault her (one finally attempting it towards the end of the film version). The father drinks himself into a stupor at a party while fantasizing about saving The Babysitter from rape by assaulting her boyfriend, and about raping The Babysitter himself. The film leaves us questioning if the only difference between fantasizing and formulating a plan is opportunity. Sex (consensual and nonconsensual) is what happens when unconscious desires become conscious manifestations, the moment fiction becomes friction. In his short story, Coover explores this with structure. There is no linearity in his writing, no marker to help the reader understand if they are in the man's fantasy world or The Babysitter's reality, so it becomes increasingly discombobulating. The men's fantasies start out soft and almost romantic in ways, talking about her scent and her blouse, but these fail to satisfy, and so the fantasies progress to the next level, becoming increasingly violent, as each of the men indulges in fetishizing The Babysitter. In particular, the father's ability to keep his desires suppressed begins to slip as he speaks sections of his fantasies out loud at the party he is attending.

The Babysitter is the perfect placement for the fantasies of men because there is an existing patriarchal power structure already enmeshed in the role — she is a young woman who has been hired for domestic services. She's available, alone, and convenient; she's nurturing and playful. She's reminiscent of a youth passed. She's young and likely inexperienced, so she isn't a threat to any man's virility and could be easier to convince. She is already a part of the father's world — the home fires burn for her. He knows the schedule of the house, when the kids will be asleep. She'll be bored, and likely there will be no rival — or, rather, saviour — for the young woman. The idea that she would protest or fight back is not usually part of the fantasy. He is the spider, she is the fly who wandered into his web.

From real life to screen — *When a Stranger Calls*, *Halloween* — all of these "babysitter in peril" films link back to the first highly publicized babysitter victim, Janett Christman, who was just three days shy of turning fourteen-years-old when she was murdered in 1950 in Columbia, Missouri, while babysitting the Romack couple's toddler, Gregory. Janett lived in an apartment above Ernie's Café and Steakhouse, her family's restaurant, where she frequently helped out. She was a responsible child who loved playing piano for the choir, and she was saving up for a new suit that she wanted for Easter. She arrived at the Romacks' at 7:30 p.m. Before leaving, as one does, Mr. Romack showed Janett where his gun was kept and taught her to load and fire it (which seems like it should have been slightly above her pay grade). He told her that under no circumstances should she open the door before first turning on the porch light and checking to see who it was through the window. At 10:30 p.m. a phone call came into the local police station. It was a frantic girl, screaming "come quick" on the other end before the phone line went dead. With no tracing abilities back then, and no address, the officer who took the call could only hang up the phone, shrug his shoulders, and hope the girl made it out okay.

The Romacks' phoned home at 11 p.m., but there was no answer, and they assumed she fell asleep. A few hours later, they returned home and found the front porch light on, the front and back door unlocked, a broken window, and their toddler safe and sound asleep upstairs. The Babysitter, though, was dead. The general consensus was that Robert Mueller, a twenty-seven-year-old mutual acquaintance of both Janett and the Romacks, had committed the assault and murder. Mueller had made sexually suggestive comments towards Janett in the past. She had been stabbed with a mechanical pencil, the same kind Mueller carried. There was no forced entry, so the police felt this was someone she would have opened the door to because he was a friend of the family. Robert Mueller had been out with the Romacks that evening, but had left for two hours partway through — to meet a doctor, he said. The doctor did not corroborate his alibi.

A friend of Janett's named Lois Terry suggested there was a possible second suspect. She had been babysitting the week before in the same area when someone knocked on the door. She looked outside the window and saw a stranger on the steps who gave her a sensation of complete unease. She refused to open the door, and eventually he left. Though the circumstantial evidence piled up, the police were never able to gather enough physical evidence against Robert Mueller to establish the burden of proof. He remained free until his death in 2006. Nobody was ever charged for the crime.

Janett's brutal murder changed the collective understanding of the babysitting job, calling into question the responsibility of a child's life being put on the shoulders of someone often too young to effectively manage in a crisis. It's a calculated risk, the teenager is young enough to do the work for cheap and still appreciate the money, and she's active enough to play with the children, but considered old enough to call for help if she needs it. Parents need personal time too.

And young teenagers are desperate for this responsibility. One of my nieces, a very eager and responsible one, when she was taking the babysitting course, asked why she needed to bring a pen to the class. "Oh!" she exclaimed, "Unless — do you think we'll learn how to perform a tracheotomy?" The independence and trust that older people put in teens, the attention they give them, the money — it's all very exciting. It is next-level playing house. Making food for the children, getting them into their jammies; she is a girl on the brink of womanhood, playing at being a woman, and that brings her into Lolita territory, a fetish that was brilliantly unpacked in *Lolita Podcast*.

These are all white girls, of course; I cannot speak from the position of someone with the lived experience of being a person of colour. But others have spoken very eloquently on how Black girlhood is seen in contrast to white girlhood. In racialized people, the idea of the coquette and depictions of innocence and girlhood are not treated or received in the same way because these girls have already been hypersexualized and fetishized by society. A white girl can wear a miniskirt and knee-highs and project naïveté, as though she is unconsciously playing with sexuality. A racialized person in the same outfit is seen as being overtly sexual.

The phone — the landline telephone — and the teenage girl are best friends. The fact that it is used against her when it is supposed to be her saviour is the irony. Pick up the phone, and there is always someone on the other end. But what if they can't get to you? What if your only safety — the phone — becomes the source of your danger. "Have you checked the children?" is the famous line from *When a Stranger Calls*, but we don't hear often about the 1993 sequel, *When a Stranger Calls Back*, a low-budget, made-for-tv movie starring Scream Queen Jill Marie Schoelen, with Carole Kane and Charles Durning reprising their roles from the 1979 original. It's not a brilliant film, far from a classic, with a ridiculous ending — the perpetrator has been using ventriloquism and *Hunger Games*–level makeup tricks to hide inside people's homes — but for 1993, this film was a rare occurrence of showing a fairly realistic portrayal of how people live with trauma. Trauma-survivor has become their identity. One works at a crisis centre, one is a trauma counsellor, one sports a classic lesbian mullet, one teaches self-defense. The original *Final Girl Support Group*, these are women helping women (which is the first role of The Babysitter, after all — she was hired to help a mother). It's infuriating that even our help and support of each other as women is something we are supposed to be afraid of. Mothers who are carrying most of the caregiving and housekeeping load at home, the ones who really need a night out, not only have to plan the date night and find a reliable babysitter, but then they are told to fear the babysitter — don't pick someone too attractive or — see Ben Affleck, Jude Law, Gavin Rossdale, Arnold Schwarzenegger, Ethan Hawke, Robin Williams — you might lose your husband to the nanny. It isn't just actors, it goes all the way to the top — there is a longstanding false rumour about President Joe Biden having met his wife, Dr. Jill Biden, when she was an underage babysitter for him and his first wife, Neilia Biden, who he went on to tragically lose in 1972, along with his one-year old daughter, when a tractor trailer collided with their car.

For me, when I was babysitting, I never had any interest in the father who would occasionally drive me the four or five blocks to my house when they got home past midnight. His complexion was ruddy and pink, like he was always on the precipice of anger. He was never inappropriate, but we would both sit in the front of his car silently stewing in that uncomfortable tension that exists between middle-aged men and The Babysitter. But the mother ...

After the children were in bed and asleep, I confess, I was a Nosy Parker. I would carry the folded laundry upstairs to put in their room and finger through her collection of silk, satin, and sequin dresses hanging in the walk-in closet. There would usually be a pile of clothing on the floor in the middle of the room, with spandex thongs and strappy garter belts. I had never seen anything like this except in the Victoria's Secret catalogues that would arrive in the mail and soon disappear under my brothers' pillows, I assumed. But the feelings that this elicited, this glimpse into adult sexuality, was disconcerting in the eroticism. To be Krystle Carrington clear, I wasn't attracted to the mother in any way. I wanted to learn from her. I was seduced by the movies I watched there, by her overt Joan Collins–esque glamour, the almost camp-like quality of her bold expression of femininity.

The children and I got along well, and we came up with regular rituals that we would do during our time together. We would play "movie theatre," and I would have them draw little movie tickets and concession stand menus and we would pop popcorn and eat candy. They would ride bikes and blow bubbles in the yard, play tag and hide-and-seek. Typical kid things. But one evening at bedtime, the daughter said something surprising about why they left their home country before suddenly clamming up. I put no thought into it because it didn't sound real, quite frankly. The gist of it was something to do with their being in hiding. I chalked it up to children telling fanciful tales and never mentioned it to the parents.

Not too long after that, my mother dropped me off at their house for my usual babysitting evening. The house from the street looked exactly like it had every other day that I had been there. My mom waved goodbye and made the ten-minute drive back to our house, as she usually did. I went to the front door and rang the bell as per tradition, but this time there was no answer. I rang the doorbell again. No answer. I knocked. I rang. No answer. I wondered if perhaps they had gone out all together instead and forgotten to contact me, but I landed with the assumption that they were just running late. It was summertime, and it was hot, but I sat on the front steps and waited. I rang the doorbell again, but nothing had changed. I decided to peek through the window to see if I could see anyone inside, and I stepped into the garden to the right of the front door. I hated stepping on plants, but I couldn't see inside otherwise.

I peered through the window to find the house was empty. Not only of people, but of everything, including all of the beautiful furniture, the artwork, the family photos, the VHS tapes, the spangled lingerie, the coq au vin, it was all gone. The floors shined like no one had ever stepped on them. Everything inside had vanished, like the legend of Brigadoon, an enchanted Scottish village that appears in the Highland mists for one day only every hundred years before disappearing again.

It felt like an exceptionally long, lonely walk home to my house. To my mother's surprise, I ran to her when I arrived home and buried myself in her Northern Reflections sweater. Confused and distraught, I explained what I had seen, or rather, not seen. She was as confused as I was. How does someone, why would someone, move away within the span of a week without telling anyone? I was terribly sad. I liked this family, this woman and these kids, and I knew I would never see them again. I was also afraid for them. Had they been involved in something dangerous that required them to run? Were they okay? I would likely never know the truth, and the not knowing was what disturbed me the most.

Every time The Babysitter walks through the doors of a new family's home, she is entering into an intimate connection not only with the children but with the adults of the home, which can be both dangerous and empowering. Connecting with mothers other than The Babysitter's own can provide excellent practical education in the various ways women parent their children, and so, like an intern, The Babysitter learns hacks and tips that she can stow away for when she has children of her own. But that intimacy also puts her directly in the path of every dysfunction that exists in that family dynamic. That's a vulnerable position for vulnerable teenagers which we don't put enough support behind.

I wondered if perhaps the child's fanciful story were true. For months, I ran through the scenarios in my mind. Maybe they were in the Witness Protection Program — was that a thing in Canada or just the United States? Maybe they were bank robbers? Outlaws on the run, like Bonnie and Clyde? Maybe an abusive ex-husband had found them, and they had decided to take off? I rationally knew that it was likely something simple like a job opportunity that had suddenly appeared, so they had to leave the country to snap it up, or a family crisis that required them to move back to their home country quickly, and they just forgot to call The Babysitter. I probably didn't mean much in the grand scheme of their world. I was just a girl who came into their house for a few hours a week.

But then one day, many months later, my phone rang, and when I lifted the receiver, I heard a little voice say "Awwwy?" It was my little friend! My dance party partner, my movie theatre usher, my pal. He said "I miss you," and I told him I missed him, too, and then suddenly, it was her. And her beautiful accent "Allyson! My sweet girl. I'm so sorry for the way we left you. I've always felt dreadful about it. Couldn't be helped. Now I can't tell you where we are, but I wanted you to know we are all okay. And just to tell you how much you meant to our family and how deeply we miss you. I wish you all the best in this world, and I hope that someday our paths will cross again."

But they never did.

THE PSYCHO CHICK

(OR, THE CULLING OF THE HEARD)

"Sometimes, the only way to stay sane
is to go a little crazy."

— *Girl, Interrupted*

Mandy Lane's eyes reminded me of the time I discovered my cat had partially eaten a mouse on my living room floor. Like an excited kid with an Oreo cookie, he only ate the middle. He had this look of comfortable nonchalance when faced with my horror. When I hollered his name, he seemed like he wasn't paying attention, his stare blank. But somehow you could tell, underneath the cool exterior — he was chuffed. Those were the eyes of bisexual spree-killer-on-a-mission Mandy Lane, from the film *All the Boys Love Mandy Lane*, the low-budget indie slasher starring Amber Heard in her first leading role.

The character of Mandy Lane is a fleshed-out trope of the girl that everyone, no matter their age, gender, or orientation, would die to get with. It questions what would happen if a young woman not only understood the power of her seductiveness but chose to willingly wield it to hurt others. The character is played by bisexual actress Amber Heard, once an "It Girl" who has since become the reviled face of a crude public horror show when her marriage to Johnny Depp turned into a public pile driving of their personal characters. Before they married, Depp was a global sensation and one of North America's highest paid entertainers, revered for being a Puck, an imp, a rapscallion. His handsome, chiselled face was transformed countless times and often expertly masked under elaborate costuming and makeup. Heard was a rising star, an ingenue; the quintessential femme fatale and the picture of the perfect blonde. A Hollywood goddess. A vamp with the blonde waves of Britney Spears, the icy stare of Megan Fox, and the sultry, simmering heat of Angelina Jolie.

Directed by Jonathan Levine (*Warm Bodies* and *Nine Perfect Strangers*), *All the Boys Love Mandy Lane* premiered at TIFF's Midnight Madness back in 2006 to positive reviews. The distribution rights were bought by convicted rapist Harvey Weinstein and The Weinstein Company. But after poor test screenings with the public, the film was stuck in the closet for years. Its unattainability became its trademark and its legendary appeal, and, like its main character, Mandy Lane, the film was deemed more attractive the more unattainable it became. While on the shelf, the film built a small cult following of both people who caught a small taste of it during the festival circuit and the people who were desperate to. It was finally released in 2013 to middling reviews — critics felt the film was too smart for a summer slasher and too simple for an art house classic; like the film's implied bisexual lead character, it flirted with both.

The film takes place in the early 2000s, with a '70s aesthetic due in part to the colouring (golds and browns), the lens flares, and the sudden blurry pauses that hang on moments of extreme violence. Its filmic elements are reminiscent of horror classics like *I Spit on Your Grave, Carrie, The Texas Chainsaw Massacre* and *The Town That Dreaded Sundown*. Its structure is that of a simple teenage slasher, and it follows the expected principles: a group of horny teenagers takes off in a pickup truck for an end-of-school weekend away at a remote holiday house. In this case, it's not a cabin in the woods, but a wide open Texan ranch that is owned by the father of the stoner character, Red. Red has invited along two cheerleaders: an anorexic, pill-popping blonde named Chloe and her buxom, nymphomaniac, brunette frenemy Marlin. Two football player friends come along for the ride: handsome fuckboy Jake and the more reserved Bird (the only character of colour). A reluctant chaperone to the weekend is chiseled thirty-something ranch hand Garth, played by Anson Mount, who would be just as home in a Hallmark film wielding an axe and chopping wood as he is patrolling the fields slinging his rifle. Red has also managed to accomplish something unheard of before in their high school: he has (through Chloe's convincing) managed to get gorgeous loner Mandy Lane to agree to come with them. And it goes without saying that anywhere Mandy goes, you can expect her devout stalker/erstwhile childhood best friend, Emmet, will be lurking in the shadows.

Nine months before this weekend, Mandy Lane had arrived for the first day of school after a scorching summer glow-up. She is a blonde, athletic, all-American girl with a pert nose and a disinterested gaze. All anyone at school can do is talk about her. The cheerleaders befriend her and use her as capital to get to the boys who leer at and drool over her in the hallways, at the bus stop, and from the bleachers as she runs track. The school quarterback can't wait to invite her to his back-to-school pool party, which Mandy agrees to go to as long as she can bring her best friend, Emmet. After what appears to be a chivalrous scuffle with the quarterback who was pawing at Mandy without her consent, Emmet convinces him to leap off the roof and into the swimming pool to impress her — his prize: cracking his skull open on the side of the pool when he misses.

Flash forward to the end of the school year, and Emmet has become a social pariah while Mandy has become even more legendary. Red tells his friends as she runs past in her short shorts and tank top, "There she is, boys, Mandy Lane. Untouched, pure. Since the dawn of junior year men have tried to possess her, and to date all have failed. Some have even died in their reckless pursuit of this angel." To these boys, she is the top of Mount Everest, the Holy Grail, Helen of Troy — not human, but a trophy to be pursued by zealots who will use every tactic to win her sexual attention as the focus of their constant hunger, fetishizing, projections, and surveillance. She is never alone. Even when Mandy is changing at home, we see it from the point of view of an unknown person standing in the bushes watching her remove her bra.

And what have we learned, class, about being the high school girl that everyone wants? Whether it's Britney Spears, Lindsay Lohan, Megan Fox, Angelina Jolie, Selena, or Amber Heard, being the object of everyone's fantasy is not magical, and it isn't a compliment. In fact, it's often a killer. I'm reminded of a satirical tweet that said, "If you've ever been described as 'lighting up every room you walk into,' you have a forty-seven percent higher chance of being brutally murdered" — well put, Yasmin. If you aren't killed by an obsessed fan (like Yolanda Saldívar, president of Selena's fan club, and her murderer), or you don't break from the pressure and turn to drugs or alcohol, then you face a social take-down, *particularly* if you are seen as a bi woman.

I'm far from famous or sought after, but I know something about bi scrutiny. In my own life, I knew my first queer relationship was going to be challenging for me to navigate given how many people seemed to want to be at the helm. Everyone seemed to have an opinion, including family, friends, and colleagues, who all seemed comfortable making jokes about this being "just a phase," or commenting on how powerful my then wife's personality was. To this day, my sister still teasingly asks me on the phone, "So, did you wake up super gay today or just a little gay?" as though the answer will change twenty years later. But other peoples' judgments around how my heart and mind functioned, and what was going on inside my own bedroom, scorched me. I knew that somehow the optics around my falling in love with a woman after an adolescence of enthusiastically "straight" dating and passionate, tumultuous relationships with men was going to be seen as surprising behaviour, and the relationship not recognized as what it actually was for me at the time, which was stabilizing and nurturing and safe.

The repeated implication was that my ex was a Machiavellian schemer who was out to convert straight women, which infuriated her, particularly when she and I both knew the truth: I was the ardent pursuer.

The character and life of the bisexual woman is often considered "crazy" and evil. We have a long and sordid history as a society of taking women who love women, fetishizing them, and then using their bisexuality as an excuse to label them as unstable, even with the other factors at play. This happens particularly with young women who are still growing and developing into human beings facing the unceasing want of society when it comes to controlling their sexuality. Their sexuality, any hint of queerness, is used as a weapon against them in the media instead of being a part of their complex nature as fully formed human beings.

In *All the Boys Love Mandy Lane*, the moment the girls retreat to the bathroom Mandy is suddenly different than she has been in the entire film. Alone with Chloe, she is gentle and caring, stroking Chloe's hair and saying she is safe with her. Mandy's hands tremble with want as she touches Chloe's face. This is not bi-performative play for the male gaze — there are no men around — but Mandy could be manipulating Chloe's desire for her to toy with her or test her. Whatever her agenda, the chemistry seems real enough that the character's potential bisexuality allows us to watch the rest of the young, straight relationships through detached eyes. What we see is not healthy behaviour.

This interaction between Chloe and Mandy is the only tenderness shown between any characters. Drunk girls in bathrooms. Supportive and caring. It's the place many young women have their first same-sex kisses. At least, it was for me, skipping away from the dance floor and stumbling into a bar bathroom stall together, giggling. There is a code around the ladies' room. It's a sanctuary, a temple, a safe haven in a dangerous world. A woman meets a drunk woman in a bathroom crying, and all of the other drunk women will read her in a second, know who has harmed her, and be prepared to go to war for her. So, when Chloe is being hunted later in the film and runs to Mandy, only to be penetrated by her knife, it's a double betrayal.

In most horror movies, I want to scream "don't go in that room," but in *All the Boys Love Mandy Lane* I want to scream to these girls, "Don't do *him*! Don't waste the few precious years of your youth dumbing yourself down and sacrificing your mind and body to teenage boys who seem to struggle to see their cis-female counterparts as humans, let alone potential partners!" I speak from the depths of my own inner teenager who spent my teen years trying unsuccessfully to find happiness in straight relationships.

Who I am, and what words I use to identify myself to others, often has me twisted in knots because it seems determined by what others think I am, or what I want others to think about the people I have loved, instead of something intrinsic to me. The labels have changed from something self-empowering to now a title that is earned, bestowed, and must be maintained at all stages of your life. I have been many people in my lifetime, at different times different labels would apply to me. That is not a sign that I have an unstable identity, it's proof that I am growing and learning.

All the Boys Love Mandy Lane is a film about the first generation to be raised on free and plentiful online porn — teenagers who are hyper-sexualized and overly focused on women's body parts. They have sex with no emotion, just to stave off boredom, or earn social capital, or to calm a fragile male ego, not for any actual connection or emotion. The boys and girls in this film treat each other in horribly selfish ways. Jake carries a map marked with all of the girls he's fucked, like they are tourist attractions. He claims he has "had" a girl in forty-two different states, and he's going up to Alaska in the summer. He refers to his regular sex-partner, Marlin, as "the well" (as in "guess it's time to go back to the well"). And when she asks for reciprocal oral sex from him, Jake laughs it off. Why would she expect him to give her pleasure? She's literally a hole to him. Bird, at first, seems like a nice guy. Instead of sexualizing Mandy, he asks to hold her hand, and she either really feels, or plays into his fantasy of her being genuinely surprised and pleased at the old-fashioned gesture. But when she consents, Bird immediately pushes it further. How about a kiss? When he's allowed a chaste kiss on the cheek, he pushes her further to make out with him.

Mandy is rescued by Garth, the ranch hand, whose purpose seems to be keeping the teenage boys in line and gazing off into the horizon with a handsome man-scowl during conversations. Halfway through the film, Garth tells the teens about how he recently had to kill forty head of cattle because they had gotten sick, and you can't sell sick animals, you have to cull them for their own good. From a moralistic perspective, it's easy to see that a "sickness" has infected these teens and they are not going to grow-up with a healthy mindset about relationships. At the end of the film, psycho killer Emmet actually corrals Chloe like a heifer, chasing her in his pickup truck across the scenic, open rural fields while she runs, exposed, clad in pink satin and lace lingerie, back to the ranch house and her death at the hands of Mandy Lane, who was in on the killings the whole time. She was not that innocent.

And that brings us to now, fifteen years after *All the Boys Love Mandy Lane*, when the world watched a court case between Amber Heard and Johnny Depp, streamed live. It was a scenario that could have been the alternate ending to Mandy's life if the character had done what was expected of her and picked the most privileged boy — the handsomest, richest, or most athletically gifted. Amber Heard chose to marry one of the most privileged men in the world and ended up in a relationship that was abusive, toxic, and disappointingly juvenile in many ways. Johnny Depp is known for developing some of the most unforgettable, eccentric, unhinged characters on film: Jack Sparrow, the Mad Hatter, Willy Wonka, Barnabas Collins, and Edward Scissorhands, all unique in appearance, but characters who share the same soul. Their exterior is child-like and naive, always a fish out of water in society. But what we *really* feed on is the rot festering under their surface. Every single one of Depp's characters in the fantasy genre holds the *potential* for extreme violence, but never tips over into it. That potential is what gives them gravitas and makes them exciting — it's a form of psychological roughhousing. Like when you were a child and you would play with your father or a goofy uncle — they pretended to be a bad guy only to pick you up in the air, flip you upside down, and shake little treasures out of your pockets. You knew, even as a child, that it could all go horribly wrong, but you trusted them not to take it there. Depp's entire acting persona is based on him walking that very thin tightrope of trust. We trust that Edward Scissorhands wouldn't actually cut someone, Jack Sparrow would never hurt Elizabeth Swann, and Willy Wonka hasn't killed children in workplace accidents. He takes it to the edge of violence, and then pulls back.

So it was no surprise, really, when Johnny Depp sued Amber Heard for defamation, for $50 million, all for writing about her experience of sexual harassment and abuse in a *Washington Post* op-ed (almost ironically at this point) titled, "I spoke up against sexual violence — and faced our culture's wrath. That has to change."

This case was not to determine who abused who. It was specifically about her essay. Depp claimed the following lines in her essay were false and defamatory: (1) "I spoke up against sexual violence — and faced our culture's wrath." (2) "Then two years ago, I became a public figure representing domestic abuse, and I felt the full force of our culture's wrath for women who speak out." (3) "I had the rare vantage point of seeing, in real time, how institutions protect men accused of abuse."

First of all, the title of an essay is often not in the hands of the author. For search engine optimization, specific keywords are used to generate essay titles to ensure they hit on the highest number of searches. Secondly, Amber Heard was literally, at the time, the Ambassador for Women's Rights at the American Civil Liberties Union. It was her *job* to be a public figure speaking about domestic abuse.

Ultimately, she lost the case, and Depp won, but the gang-up on her was devastating and horrible to witness.

Domestic violence is not simple. Very few people who are verbally, psychologically, or physically terrorized are completely passive. People often try every tactic they can think of to protect themselves. And when it goes on for years and the relationship becomes irreparable and it has taken a psychological toll on your mind, it is not unusual for someone to fight back or even meet their abuser's behaviour and become abusive themselves.

It's not new for an abused person to be blamed as the instigator when they fight back against their own abuse, or to have the relationship be called "mutually abusive." *Vanity Fair* tweeted the day of Tina Turner's death about her "tumultuous relationship" with Ike Turner, a man who Tina described in her autobiography as someone who "threw hot coffee in my face, giving me third-degree burns," and who "used my nose as a punching bag so many times that I could taste blood running down my throat when I sang. He broke my jaw. And I couldn't remember what it was like not to have a black eye." Even the great Tina Turner is not immune from society's determination to balance the scales somehow between abuser and abused, by downplaying the abuse in the relationships with euphemisms. The onus to be the bigger person is always on the part of the wronged person. The implication being that the abused partner should feel responsible for keeping their abuser calm at all times, 24/7, mollycoddling them into constant submission. If you have had the unfortunate experience of being with a verbally or physically abusive person, you know that the temperature in the room changes swiftly and without warning.

The only other socially acceptable option given to women is leaving their abuser. But getting out of their way is not so simple. Leaving is logistically complicated. Tina Turner had to bolt out of a roadside hotel with thirty-six cents in her pocket and almost got hit by a truck on the freeway as she fled. Not to mention that the days after a partner leaves a marriage is the most dangerous time of all for them because the abuser is forced to confront the consequences of their actions. An abuser will use every control tactic they have in their arsenal to force their partner to comply with their wishes.

The clinical psychologist Dr. Dawn Hughes, who examined Amber Heard for twenty-nine hours, said that having been raised in a family with domestic violence "she learned that she could love someone who hurts her. She knew that people who hurt her also could love her." An abusive person is not a villain every single day of their lives. And sometimes, the relationship isn't abusive until it's over. CBC News reported that sixty percent of intimate partner violence occurs *after the relationship has ended*. It's the abuser's way to get the relationship to continue on any terms, even negative ones, because often the alternative — abandonment, failure, isolation, lack of control, rejection, facing the personal issues that led to the end of the relationship — is too painful for their fragile sense of self to bear.

Amber Heard faced death threats and was armchair diagnosed with mental health issues and personality disorders. She was called a liar, a gold digger, a drug addict. Most humiliatingly, she had her name linked to grotesque rumours that she had defecated on their bed as a "prank," and sharing the hashtag #AmberTurd was encouraged. It was the most juvenile of all juvenile court proceedings, with Johnny Depp, a nearly sixty-year-old man, snickering and mugging for cameras. I suspect in another fifteen years, we will look back on this time as shamefully as we do with the images of Britney lashing back at paparazzi with an umbrella.

In the film, it's easy to see why Mandy Lane wouldn't be interested in any of the high school boys. Mandy is intense, focused, not like the normal kids. She doesn't fit their mould. A point *could* be made that Mandy Lane is a volcel (portmanteau of *voluntary* and *celibate*) because she refuses to show any interest in the group's teenage sexual hedonism. Or, she may have just been a little ahead of her time. Across the board, studies are finding that young people are having less sex these days. Jean M. Twenge, a psychology professor from San Diego State

University, told *The Atlantic* last year that people in their early twenties are on track to be two and a half times more likely to be abstinent than Gen Xers, and to have fewer sex partners than the two preceding generations. In another study out of University College London, social scientists found that teens were also engaging in far less sexual activity now compared to their counterparts of the '80s and '90s.

And, it turns out, more and more women are choosing voluntary celibacy for a variety of reasons: to control their own sexual narrative, to reject unequal power dynamics, and because they are busy experiencing life and not focused on others' needs. None of which is surprising to me, when finding a partner has become the nightmare that is online dating, full of lurking, unsolicited dick pics, and scary men who move from compliments to violent threats in seconds. Even if you choose to participate in heterosexual hookup culture, there is little payoff for women (who are also accepting the most risk), with only four percent of hookups yielding an orgasm for them. The focus is still on the masculine partner's release and the female's ability to provide that release. Not that an orgasm is the only reason for engaging in sex, but it is one of the more enjoyable parts.

In a movie with a high body count, Mandy Lane only directly kills two people in the film, Chloe and Emmet. Mandy's kills are personal: the two people she was intimate with. Emmet's kills are different: he kills because he can't be intimate with anyone. Emmet is an *incel*, a word originally created by a Canadian woman known only as Alana for "Alana's Involuntary Celibacy Project," to describe the unique loneliness of being partnerless for the majority of your life. The term was co-opted by violent, angry men and has now become somewhat of an ideology, although without the same complex thought behind most ideologies. To these men, sex is a form of currency, and they are poverty stricken.

Several loud voices have terrifyingly called for *sexual redistribution* or *enforced monogamy* as a way to deal with this, meaning some governing body or intense and condoned societal pressures would intervene and partner women with single men. Women reduced to forced sexual providers. Calmer voices suggest we increase sex workers as a "simple fix." Every solution presented requires controlling women's sexuality and forcing them to give in to these men. Sex workers are *human beings*, not soldiers at the frontline to be sacrificed to violent, angry men, and sex will not appease them. Incels are not angry because they aren't having sex, they are angry because they believe they should be able to control women's sexuality. Women's rejection of them amplifies their own impotence in this realm — rejection like, say, open laughter, or mockery in the form of a published article.

Emmet sees himself as the Travis Bickle character from *Taxi Driver*, "a man who stood up against the scum, the cunts, the dogs, the filth, the shit." But Mandy Lane understood that Emmet's manifesto was worthless, and he was just as much a part of the problem; "I never read it anyways," she claims, in an open and clear rejection of his male wisdom.

Mandy Lane, who has only ever been seen by her peers as an entity, a fantasy, a doll — never a real live girl — resorts to using violence to make her point. Mandy has no intention of going through with Emmet's ultimate plan of a double suicide. He stamps his feet and screams, demanding that she die with him. Instead, she beats him to death with a giant log, saying, "I think I'll finish high school first."

Amber Heard is now thirty-seven and has been apart from Depp since 2017. She is a mother now, responsible for raising a daughter, and the lessons she teaches her about relationships will inevitably be tainted by this experience. Whoever is culpable, much of Heard's thirties have been spent paying for relationship decisions made in her twenties. Her youth was spent dodging assaults not only from her partner but from all of us as well.

When a woman is driven to fight back against powerful forces under that much scrutiny and focus — it often does not look pretty. And when we only ever wanted them to look pretty, looking ugly is sometimes their only salvation.

THE VICTIM

(IT'S COMPLEX)

"I have been to hell and back. And let
me tell you, it was wonderful."

— LOUISE BOURGEOIS

An old friend lost her husband when a complication arose during what was supposed to be a fairly risk-free surgery. She was, naturally, shocked and then devastated. Friends brought muffins and flowers for the first week or two. Everyone enjoyed the wake, which instead of a sombre church affair, included gin martinis, cigars, and piano music (he would have wanted it that way), but after the celebration of his life, her life as the surviving spouse had to go on without him, which felt terribly unfair. A month or two later, while she was out front of their long-time home tending the garden, her ninety-year-old neighbour shuffled by, dressed in black head to toe, still mourning her own husband who had died decades ago. She hugged my freshly grieving friend, cupped her face gently with a nod and sigh before saying, "No one cares."

She wasn't wrong. The cult of happiness still wages strong. We crave happy. We maniacally search it out to the exclusion of all other experiences. We promote peoples' ability to survive trauma unscathed, and then we expect it of them and of ourselves. Whether it is grief, sorrow, clinical depression, or complex trauma, we say on one hand we will be there for our friends and family while simultaneously offering advice like "chin up," "keep calm and carry on," and "don't worry, be happy." Kick yourself. Keep moving. In my own family of origin, there was little time for wallowing or indulging in our sorrows. An emotional child, I was frequently called Sarah Bernhardt after a curly haired French stage actress from the late nineteenth and early twentieth century who was known for playing overly maudlin tragic parts (an iconic pose of hers was draping herself over a fainting couch with the back of her hand to her forehead). Far from being a victim, though, Sarah Bernhardt, after a decades-long incredibly successful career, reportedly collapsed during a dress rehearsal and briefly awoke from a coma to ask, "When do I go on?"

There is no such thing as too happy, but you sure can be too sad. The gatekeeping I have personally witnessed and experienced around the amount of sadness or frustration that society rations out to someone when they have been injured or mistreated includes definite social parameters: don't be too maudlin; watch with whom you express your emotions; don't hyperfixate on your troubles; don't include anger in your grieving process; don't put anything in writing; don't let your children see you cry; and don't let your grief affect your productivity for too long. In other words — please, go ahead and be sad, but don't wave it around in our faces or make it our problem.

Friends want to be there for you, but sadness is messy. Sadness wakes you up at 4 a.m. and won't let you go back to sleep. The worse the trauma, the more it is like drowning: You threaten to bring down anyone who touches you. Others may throw you a line, but they will keep their distance. I had a few friends vanish during my divorce process, claiming they began fighting with their own spouses or feeling insecure because they had the same stresses, the same problems, and the same communication style in their own marriage. Would they be abandoned too? Or they left when they grew impatient with how frequently I cancelled plans with them. They found me to be a bit of a downer ruminating on perceived betrayals, or they felt uncomfortable with the awkward teenage stage divorcées go through when they start dating again. As I get older, I notice that the more bad things that have happened in the course of my lifetime (experiencing violence, multiple miscarriages, financial stresses, illness, adultery, divorce, deaths, depression), the smaller my supportive circle has become.

"No one cares," I could say, but I try not to blame, resent, or judge anyone who walks away from my table. People come and go, and my personal lifelong goal is to learn to let them go with grace. It's understandable that the sad, traumatized, or grieving person is not fun to be around. And one person's trauma can trigger a lot of pain in another. I have friends who can't be around people with alcohol or substance abuse because it triggers their own past issues or experiences with abusive family members. Sometimes, self-preservation conflicts with supporting the survival of others.

With the exception of a minuscule number of incredibly lucky or privileged people, the human experience is to constantly torment and victimize each other. I think that fact is very hard for our collective unconscious to appreciate. We could centre our conversations about trauma around putting every conflict into perspective, acknowledging the pain caused, supporting the trauma, treating the causes, repairing the relationships, and finding ways to prevent conflict from happening again, but instead we instead have chosen to throw up our hands and sanctimoniously say, "Well, some kinds of people are just determined to have a victim mentality." It takes the onus off of those doing the tormenting when we can quantify a person's suffering on our own scale instead of understanding theirs.

A person with a victim complex, by definition, is someone who has suffered through hard times or trauma but not developed a healthy way to cope, instead developing a negative view of life in which they feel they have no control over what happens to them. In other words — a person with a victim complex is *an actual victim* who has not processed their complex trauma and still feels out of control. Yet we choose to both despise victims while also holding them in the highest regards in our film and literature.

You probably know her as a *final girl*, a term that was created by Carol J. Clover in her book entitled *Men, Women, and Chain Saws*. "She is the one who encounters the mutilated bodies of her friends and perceives the full extent of the preceding horror and her own peril; who is cornered, wounded; whom we see scream, stagger, fall, rise, and scream again. She is abject terror personified." The final girl is the perfect victim, the foil for the monster. She is the only character who presents a challenge to her unrelenting pursuer. The final girl might get knocked down, but she gets up again and again and again. She uses what knowledge she has gained in every battle to fight back harder and stronger. She might pull together a rag-tag crew of supporters, but she will inevitably watch as, one by one, over sequels, they are all taken out and only she remains.

Each name the term conjures in your mind is likely a white woman from a big budget franchise: Sidney Prescott from *Scream*, Laurie Strode from *Halloween*, Ellen Ripley from *Alien*, or Sarah Connor from *Terminator*. These women are the victims we love and cheer for — the perfect frontier-style, capable, white women who evolved from being a victim into being the heroines of their franchises and became something more akin to a huntress, a person who dedicates their existence to taking down a single threat. Victims can only stay socially acceptable victims for a short period of time before we want them to follow the way of the hero and emerge from their trauma with new strength and wisdom. Final girls have to fight and live their way through the trauma to be respected. Paradoxically, we want people who are at their weakest to be the strongest they have ever been.

I was the victim of assault more than one time in my adult life. A long time ago, in my twenties, and then again in my forties. Some people would consider the most recent assault minor. But for me, it wasn't. There were complicated circumstances around it that made this "minor" action majorly terrifying. The person who perpetrated it was on the front page of the newspaper four days afterwards being sought out by the police as a suspect in a string of (unrelated) crimes. He was arrested, imprisoned awaiting trial, and released after a trial due to lack of evidence. My shock and the fear which has continued to visit me years later has had implications on every aspect of my life.

I would like to say that I became a huntress — that I fought back and became an advocate for women, and dedicated my life to supporting the abused — but I didn't because I was frightened. I'm still frightened. I was a terrible victim. I talked about it too much, and I could see people's expressions change like we all have with the macabre interest of someone observing a car wreck to sheer horror when we see the damage. I experienced a recurrence of my anxiety disorder and had panic attacks and agoraphobia for a while. And then I stopped talking about it at all. The only socially acceptable expression of women's trauma is in entertainment. There, our stories are stripped of the complexity of our inner lives and are boiled down to the one valuable thing we have to offer viewers — the unflinching endurance of female pain.

The evolved final girl, once transformed into the huntress, has no time for romance or personal interests. Men are assessed, considered, possibly used for a psychological break, and are then discarded. The huntress may even become a mother, but that role isn't something she can take the time to enjoy. Laurie Strode's version of mothering is preparing her daughter for the inevitable battle with the devil that is Michael Myers: "I have tried to protect you and prepare you. Now we have to hunt him down." Even if she loses her children, the huntress doesn't take the time to grieve because she is laser-focused on her mission — to destroy the one true evil that is stalking her. She may be a victim of the monster, but she won't succumb to seeing herself as one — that would be the real tragedy, we are meant to assume. Unlike the pretty, drunk, party girls at the sorority house, this victim will go on to remember what happened to her in perfect detail.

She is sexless to the monster. Any sexual objectification of the huntress — watching her stroke her kitty cat while wearing tight underpants, or slowly panning over her body as she does arm curls in a black tank top — is on the part of the viewer. Often, at some point in the franchise, the huntress will even change her look to defeminize herself, wearing baggy clothes, shaving her head, or masculinizing her body through weight-lifting. Her femininity doesn't define her, even if it is the thing that is drawing the monster to assault her. Sarah Connor is originally targeted because she is going to give birth — she is a potential mother. Laurie Strode is first targeted because she is a babysitter. Ripley is (arguably) targeted because she is *not* a mother and is a working woman. Sidney is first targeted because she is a daughter. There is no way to get around it. Whatever your experience of womanhood, you could be a target. The monsters that they chase don't see their humanity or under-stand their circumstances, and yet they are intimately close to them. As Ripley says to the Xenomorph almost lovingly, as one would to a lost lover or a close family friend, "You've been in my life so long, I can't remember anything else." The violence these women are battling is distinctly domestic, even if the aggressor is not family.

From life-altering government decisions to daily micro-aggressions, when I go out into the world, despite having become middle-aged, overweight, and sometimes on the arm of another woman, I am still inevitably dodging street harass-ment. A long time ago, I decided ignoring it was the safest option. But eighty percent of the time ignoring it still results in hurled obscenities — "Bitch," "Cunt," "Pussy." The only difference through the years is that the demographic of the assaulter has changed. They are older now. Sixty-year-old men sitting together on a bench rubbing their thumb and middle finger together while whistling at me like I am a cat, "Psst. Psst. Psst." Crossing the street to tell me they find me attractive, and would I accompany them for coffee? Yelling "nice tits" as I get out of a taxi, following me into a store only to call me a bitch when I walk back out, asking me if it's really "wet down there" with a lascivious smile when I cross a puddle. One time, not so long ago, a well-dressed man (who must have been over ninety) in a suit and a cocked fedora shuffled with his walker from the old folks' home across the street from my house. He even put one finger up to tell me to wait for him, so I did. I waited patiently. It took him several minutes to navigate the curb, shuffle across the two lanes, allow a car to pass, and then navigate the second curb and approach my front garden where I was watering the lawn standing next to my dog. What was so important he wanted to tell me? "Nice looking bitch. And the dog isn't bad either." With a wink. Maybe that one isn't considered harassment because I laughed. My reflex aside, the message is the same. The misogyny of Michael Myers will still be there at ninety, chasing Laurie Strode down the street, both of them in adult diapers and shuffling behind walkers.

These final girls are revered for their ability to keep taking the abuse and coming back for more. They are martyrs for the cause. There would be no movie if Ripley just threw down her flamethrower and said, "I'm done — you guys take it from here." She knows that it is her job to keep fighting because, just like moms cleaning out the fridge, she knows if she doesn't do it, nobody else is going to, and it's just going to be a bigger nightmare the next time the door gets opened. But it's problematic;

although it seems inspiring to see a bazooka across Linda Hamilton's sculpted shoulder, her gaze steely behind her aviators, we are still participating in a scenario where a woman is routinely assaulted and tortured, and we are praising that system.

As Clover writes, the final girl "is an agreed upon fiction [for] male-viewers' use of her as a vehicle for his own sadomasochistic fantasies." We think we are watching something good for us, but at the same time, what we are watching is perpetuating the idea that a strong woman can "take it" and weak women give up. The final girl's focus, while impressive in its single-mindedness, is still entirely guided by the monster's wants and desires. He wants her attention, and he gets it. In *Alien*, even though the Xenomorphs' leader is feminized as a Queen, and the species itself is canonically neither male nor female, the premise is distinctly male — a creature with a giant ridged phallus for a head whose entire existence relies on interspecies rape. Even if the misogyny that follows her is systemic in the form of a government agency that's trying to regulate her body and possible pregnancy, the huntress can't focus on anything else in her life but this one dysfunctional dynamic.

Domestic abuse that women suffer is real, hard to navigate, unique to each person, and yet we judge and deny victim status to some women every day if they are not the right kind of victim. We compare and contrast and say if one focuses their life on overcoming their traumas, and they fight for change, then they are heroic — like Elizabeth Smart, who is beautiful, well spoken, educated, religious, and has a positive mental attitude. She survived an unthinkable ordeal and has used her pain to help others. She continues to advocate for victims but believes dwelling in the past is unproductive. Interestingly, her story has been told through the eyes of men three times — by her father, an uncle, and a Mormon Republican Congressman who co-wrote her memoir.

Amanda Knox faced public scorn for considering herself a victim of an unjust system that held her imprisoned in Italy for a murder she says she did not commit. She certainly suffered. Knox has also gone on to become an author, an activist, and a journalist. Both she and Smart are centring their professional lives, personas, and identities around the trauma they faced as victims.

Unfortunately, once you have had one very upsetting thing happen to you, you seem to open a portal in the universe for multiple upsetting things happening to you, and complex trauma can be a very messy thing to sort out.

We even turn victims into pop culture pin-ups, a phenomena seen most disturbingly in little JonBenét Ramsey, the six-year-old beauty pageant winner, the image of whose *Dynasty*-sized curled hair and bright pink lipstick-covered smile is burned into our collective consciousness. We sexualize victims like Dorothy Stratten, the Playboy Playmate whose murder by her abusive, controlling boyfriend was made into the film *Star 80*. We seem to be most heartbroken by the pregnant mother victim, Sharon Tate and Laci Peterson. Or the child victim, Bella and Celeste Watts (and their pregnant mother, Shanann). Again, all of these victims are white and middle class; truthfully, other than a small handful of people, we mostly forget the women that experience violence daily. BIPOC and Trans women who have faced violence and oppression and gone missing and been murdered every day for generations continue to fight the system and protest and try to raise awareness while screaming into the void. We don't want to look at those final girls as the same kind of victim in our hierarchy because it reminds us that in their stories, *we* are the relentless monsters. Even good-natured Canadians. We never, ever, ever want to admit to being the villain. As much as we want to cover it with a smiling mask, Canada has a horrifying history.

Few people are trained in how to support complex trauma in others. Empathy can really only go so far when helping someone through a period of grief or complex PTSD or reparations for intergenerational trauma.

Complex trauma has also been referred to as combat fatigue, which is something that all of our huntresses would be experiencing. They are the brain and body's natural responses to being in a heightened state of long-lasting or repeated trauma over months or years. People with c-PTSD may dissociate, have periods when they black out, they may be reckless or destructive, sometimes violent. They often have a hard time with self-loathing and stay in abusive relationships or turn to isolation. They may be preoccupied with revenge fantasies or obsessed over religion, they may turn away from their beliefs, they may numb pain with drugs and alcohol, self-harm, or generally avoid emotions or reminders of their trauma. They often reject help and keep fighting the world on their own.

We idolize the huntress as the ultimate victim. The woman who keeps fighting until there is no fight left in them and they die or disappear. And even then, someone usually comes along to resurrect them and bring them right back into the same fight. Her story is one of the very few women-centred tales that men will pay to watch in a movie theatre. More than any other character in literature, we line up behind the victim

— we love her, fetishize her, we are saddened by her, our hearts broken by her if she is one way, and if she's another we judge her, hate her, disbelieve her, and punish her. And if we are even somewhat complicit in her victimization, we will help the perpetrators bury her and never speak of her again. Because in those cases, the ones where we are the monsters, it turns out that we don't care.

THE COVEN

(OR, IT'S NOT ABOUT WITCHCRAFT, IT'S ABOUT THE FRIENDSHIPS)

"It's the intensity of the friendship
that concerns me."

— *Heavenly Creatures*

My youngest daughter was in the middle of a transformation, changing from her long-time French immersion school to a new one that was a more traditional English public school, and she was a nervous little tween. For a child who didn't like change, the new routine, new teachers, and new rules made her want to grab her cat, disappear under her covers, and never go back to school. Add a whole global pandemic to the equation, and it was understandable. She already knew several of the girls in her class, so she had a group of friends, and for the most part they seemed bursting at the seams to see each other. Every school day seemed to be full of made-up languages, the memorizing of complex and mystifying group dances filmed around a cell phone, and eruptions in raucous cackling. But alongside that, as it so often is for preteen girls, every day there was always some transgression creating conflict and spawning an emotional injury, hot tears, and the most serious statements of all — the revoking of invitations to future birthday parties. If you were to stir the pot up and boil their fights down to the core, the cause was almost always about exclusion. There is an obsession that little girls have with being popular, and it's a psychological safety net. There is safety in a coven (a collection of individuals with similar interests). Unless, that is, your friends are actually your enemies, and you just haven't been paying close enough attention. My head would spin around the number of times the girl she seemed to be the tightest with would suddenly turn on her and become her worst enemy, and then back again, all within the span of days. From best friend to bully and right back again.

One day, when she was feeling upset about yet another drama with her friends, I took her to the playground near our home so she could transform some of her energy from negative into kinesthetic. Across the street from the playground, we noticed a new store was opening up; brown butcher paper was taped up in the windows, hiding whatever was happening inside. I reminded my daughter that I would always be there for her and that she will never be alone. But I knew there was no magic spell that would make elementary school or female friendship easier. I told her to be patient and trust that although sometimes it takes a long time to find the community that completely understands you, eventually she will. And it will all come together for her.

That's the understanding in the original version of *The Craft*, a queer-coded cult favourite from 1996. In it, four outcast girls find kindred spirits and unlimited power when they pool their energy. They begin to dress alike, to try on each other's hairstyles. They find it easy to carry each other's weight with just the tip of a finger when they put their hands together. Miracles are materialized in their shared thoughts. Fairuza Balk's iconic Nancy Downs is the most overtly queer-coded — a simmering bisexual goth girl, represented by the fire element, whose sense of self just needed a little stoking to become impossible to control. The intensity of her obsession and jealousy over Sarah, and her fury when she feels betrayed by her, puts her directly in the "angry young lesbian" trope. Consumed by angst on the inside and all spiked collars and zippers on the outside, Nancy is impossible to get close to without getting hurt. At one point in the film, Nancy goes so far as to turn herself into Sarah and seduce Sarah's paramour, Chris. "She's a witch, too, you know," Nancy says of Sarah to Chris, but she may as well be saying "She's a dyke too." When Chris suggests Nancy might be jealous, she screams, "You don't even exist to me," before her unhinged moment of shaking her head while floating on the tips of her pointed-toed leather boots chanting, "He's sorry! He's sorry! He's sorry *my ass!*" and telekinetically tossing him out the window. She is so charged by her power that she can literally walk on water.

After the murder of Chris, the girls turn on each other, ganging up first on Sarah and then Nancy as they use their collective power to bully and terrorize each other. By the end of the film, Sarah's "goodness" has won out, and Nancy ends up strapped to a bed in a mental health facility, bloody scratches across her face, trying to convince a nurse that she has the power to fly, cackling like a witch. "You don't want to become like Nancy," as Sarah says.

This is the thing that the original version of *The Craft* captured that *The Craft: Legacy* from 2020 did not. In *Legacy*, the villain (David Duchovny) says, "The thing about girls with power is they are too weak to use it against each other" — but that's patently false. Women since time immemorial (particularly white women) have wielded what little power they have to raise themselves up and push other women down instead of focusing their rage on their shared oppressors. In *Legacy*, at first it appears that their intersectionality as a group comprising a trans woman, a Black woman, a Jewish woman, and a white woman, is what brings them their power. A message that is on point for modern feminism, but it doesn't play out well in this case because, although it's a film praising the power of intersectional feminism, the story is still frustratingly centred on the white female character who uses their combined power to further her own desires. *The Craft* originally came out in 1996, smack dab in the middle of a decade filled with films about obsessive young women and their one-on-one friendships turning them into murderous bisexuals, like *Heavenly Creatures, Poison Ivy, Single White Female, Mulholland Drive, Wild Things, Bound,* and more. But there is something different about the incredible intersectional force created when diverse women connect and combine their power, as co-creator of *American Horror Story: Coven* Ryan Murphy knows well. A coven of witches is canonically queer (and, let's face it, white — think *The Witches of Eastwick, Practical Magic*).

There's connection in a coven, a group, a subculture, a place to shine incandescently. They are outsiders to society and are sometimes burned for it. They stand up for each other because, most importantly, they know they are not only stronger together, but their very survival may also depend on the strength of their coven community. Covens can communicate through thoughts or simple decorative symbols alone, which is something queer people have been doing since the hanky code was developed in the 1970s in New York City. Even before that, lesbians were known to wear their keys on a certain side of their pants as a signal. Of course, it isn't just queer people who have learned to code their existence. Whether it's a ring, tattoos, vests, bandanas, hand gestures or painted fingernails, many marginalized people find ways to subtly identify themselves to their community, and to lean on that combined strength should things go awry. Typically, this is for people from the same community, but in a coven, there is the unique opportunity to bring people from all walks of life together, sharing and leveraging each other's strengths.

In both films *The Craft* and *The Craft: Legacy*, however, there is a feminine gatekeeping of identity that I have experienced first-hand within both all-female group dynamics and queer communities, and my daughter was learning it at school already. There are rules and expectations to being in a group of women that you already know by the time you are in grade three. If you cross a line, you will inevitably be punished or shunned by the group. That attitude extends into the more toxic side of queer culture as well, from the trans-exclusionary radical feminists (or TERFs) trying to impose their definition of womanhood, to the hierarchical lesbians who work on a pyramid structure with "gold stars" at the top. There are many essays' worth of explanations as to their reasons, but the consequence is always: follow their rules, and you will be accepted into the culture; don't, and be banished. There is not a lot of room or patience for the lifetime of complex histories, stories, and backgrounds of people when it comes to exclusive access into certain communities. And when you are already ostracized from other places and spaces, struggling to find acceptance in the community you want to connect with feels particularly painful.

In *The Craft* we see witchcraft as wish-fulfillment. They cast spells geared to bring them what they each desire most: love, revenge, beauty, and power. They are little girls' dreams: the love of a prince even if he is enchanted into falling for her, revenge against oppressors, impossible beauty standards, and being crowned the most powerful in the land. But so easily, the fairest in all the land can turn into the evil queen, as magic has a dark side.

Another day back at the playground with my daughter, another girl-fight. I watched as she climbed the big rope spider-web and flipped upside down on the monkey bars. But she loved, most of all, when I pushed her on the swing. My palm firmly on her back, I told her I'm sorry about her troubles, and she flew up and came back into my waiting hands. I pushed her up again and told her to keep being her best self. I continued to catch her and push her away. Remember to let everyone play together. Catch her. Remember to be inclusive. Push. Turn the other cheek when they are petty. Catch. Remember the relationship first — tell them you care. Push. Tell them how you want to be treated. Catch. Remember to empathize.

Give them a boost, send them off, and then pull them back in when they are hurting — so much of motherhood is looped in this cycle.

She was still upset, and so we went across the street to visit the new store. The butcher paper had come down to reveal an old-world magic shop with a gas lamp hanging out front of a glossy black door with lead glass windows. Inside, cauldrons sat high atop the bookshelves, stirred by long wooden spoons, without human intervention. The ceiling was a giant clock, with an intricate design of gold leaf stars and circles. The bookshelves were lined with Edward Gorey illustrated books, an *Atlas of Cursed Places*, and *The Seasonal Soul: A Mystic's Guide to Inner Transformation*.

I tried to steer her away from the Harry Potter series to find something a little less mainstream, authors who are less hurtful, women who don't build worlds and use them to destroy others. They sold faux spell books and charms and vintage toys and candles, and my daughter was delighted. I bought her and her sister a copy of *The Little Witch's Book of Spells* and brought them to the counter where the two cashiers warmly welcomed us. My littlest was not afraid to open up to people, and she told the cashiers that she had a reason to buy a spell book. She was hoping there would be a spell in it to help her connect with her friends better and protect her from bullies at her new school.

The two cashiers got to work immediately surrounding her with positive energy. My daughter radiated a glowing happiness as they heaped words of praise over her, telling her how charming she is and that she needn't be afraid. "Because you see," the dark-haired one said, raising her hand to the side of her mouth in an exaggerated stage whisper, "we are witches."

She opened the spell book in front of my daughter and showed her a page that recommended you write your bully's name on paper, slip it into a Tupperware container full of water, and stick it in your freezer. "That will freeze your bully's behaviours," she explained. "But in case that doesn't work, here's a spell from me." She pulled a business card out of her desk and waved her hand over it clockwise in a circle. She slipped the business card inside the copy of the children's book we were buying and explained, "I've put a protection spell on the card. You hide this in your pocket and bring it to school with you. It will keep you safe. The good news is that you can share this card with a friend who might need protecting too. *But* promise me that if it doesn't work, and you are still feeling scared, that you will come back in here with your mom and see me, okay?" In that moment, I was simply grateful for these women stepping in to help my daughter, even in this unconventional way. There is only so much you can do when parenting alone.

As we walked out the door the dark-haired one said, "Remember, you can come here anytime, you don't even need to buy anything. You are safe here." And for the first time since my separation, I started to think maybe we are safe. Maybe the fear I've had for so long was a false assumption that I was parenting my daughters alone. We have been surrounded this whole time by the women who came before us, the ones who tell us their stories and share their winnings and send up flares and warnings. Women are trailblazers, showing us the safest pathways through this world. Their lives and deaths and their good and bad experiences all matter. And it has a lasting impact on our daughters and our sons and everyone all along the rainbowed gender spectrum. It's hard to tell this to my daughters, though.

A mother's words, though soothing, don't always have the effect you want them to. Often, the words of another woman, one or more, have more resonance.

EPILOGUE

LOVE IS DIGGING THE GRAVE

"[Grief] occupies the core of our being and extends through our fingers to the limits of the universe. Within that whirling gyre all manner of madness exists; ghosts and spirits and dream visitations, and everything else that we, in our anguish, will into existence."

— NICK CAVE

Everything fades away in time, memories especially. Through the years, there have been moments with my children that I try to burn into my memory. I will say to myself, "Remember right now, her tiny hand can wrap around your thumb," and as the years go by, I can remember repeating the words, I can conjure up an image of my first baby's tiny little hand wrapped around my finger, but I can't recreate the powerful sensation of love and joy that I felt. The memory always pales in comparison to the experience. That frightens me more than anything. How quickly and completely I have lost the most important moments about being a mother. Some of the most monumental moments that I swore, as the guardian of their infancies, that I would keep sacred — their first steps, their first words, and the funny way they pronounced them. The tiny little things those tiny little kids did. But no matter how hard I try to keep them all, the memories are vanishing. I think I need to be compassionate with myself; vanishing is something mothers need to accept.

My own mother disappeared from my life slowly. She had a rare, progressive, degenerative neurological disease, and every day we seemed to lose another piece of her. First to go was her ability to do a little soft-shoe in the kitchen while she cooked, and then she struggled to really cook at all. When she drove her car into my father's office (through an exterior wall), she stopped driving, and when she had a drop attack and rolled down a hill while picking up the grandkids from school, she stopped doing that too. Soon, she couldn't manage stairs by herself. She would scoot her way down on her bum, just like I was teaching my toddler to do at home at the time, but then we determined that wasn't safe either. My father, who had been by her side since they were children themselves, refused to accept that she couldn't sleep in their second-floor bedroom and would carry her up their sweeping staircase to their room every night. But it was clear to us all that she was leaving us, painfully slowly, which she finally did on my birthday in 2023, slipping away in her sleep.

Most people with her illness survive a few years at best. She made it over a decade, thanks to the incredible care she received from my eighty-eight-year-old father who was beside my mother for eighty-two years. They met in a split grade one-two class and became best friends, and then eventual sweethearts and spouses. With his love and her incredible, dedicated PSWs, she thrived physically and psychologically. By the end, she was immobile. She could grasp a spoon, but had to be fed. She hovered above the ground in a stork-like sling to be transferred by machine from her wheelchair to bed. Her mind was still entirely intact, though. She had the words, she just couldn't get them out. She remembered the dance, she just couldn't get her brain to move her feet.

Mom used to have the same dream every night. "Boring!" Dad would say teasingly. He dreams in Technicolor, he's a celebrity on the red carpet, or exploring the outer reaches of space. For Mom, once a dedicated teacher, she was always back in Winnipeg in front of her grade one class. She remembers the names of every child she ever taught. Her dream always ends the same, with her buttoning up their coats to send them home at the end of the day.

Mom didn't dictate to us or lecture. She was a teacher, so she taught us lessons, but you had to pay attention to pick up on them because they often came by example. Love without fences, help without question. Trust in the inherent goodness of the people around you, and they will be good to you in return. The world can be changed through billions of small acts of support from one person to another and compassion first. And of course, perhaps most importantly, feed your community to make it stronger. Mondays were Meals on Wheels day. Wednesdays she cooked for shut-ins and for grief-stricken families at funerals, and she made free lunch for the members of Alcoholics (not so) Anonymous who had lunch in the church hall weekly. On Saturdays, she managed the community food bank. Mom never told me about her own dreams. I don't know if she wanted to be a famous dancer or if she just liked moving her body to music. I wish I knew. But I know she liked to feed people, and she remembered all of our stories. So, I try to remember the important ones for my children. Like the time, a few years ago, when a red bird landed in our backyard.

"There's a red bird outside! A red bird!" I heard my daughter shrieking, like the bird had landed on our deck from outer space instead of a nearby branch. I had been perched on my last nerve all afternoon. Our day was busy, and I had overcommitted myself as usual. I had been watching a friend's daughter for hours already, and I had planned a special night out for us all during the never-ending pandemic. Something that was completely safe, secluded, and yet surrounded with people and excitement. Faces weren't washed. Hair remained unbrushed. The snacks weren't even packed yet. I wanted to shout with profound sarcasm, "A bird — outside?! No! You don't say?!" but I love my daughter, so I stopped what I was doing, I looked and listened, even though we should have been in the car by then. We were late for the fun (an old Elvira Kurt joke) at the drive-in movie, and I love drive-in movies. "The cat got it!" She had buried the lede but now delivered it breathlessly and with razor-sharp punctuation. I wanted to shout an expletive because I did not have time for this, but I was aware that I am constantly being watched by my children. Whether I liked it or not, I was going to have to instantly create a learning moment for us all on how to handle a crisis.

Stay calm. Keep a sharp eye out. Assess the situation to see if you need outside help (how does one perform mouth-to-beak on a bird?). The wounded should always be the most worked-up person in the room, not the rescuers (so why were we all flailing around?). Be the leader if there isn't a clear one. And if you are going to lead, then lead with love. But love is hard to teach. Where to even start?

Love is gentle. I coaxed the cat out of the way and put my hand out for the small, trembling body of what turned out to be a fiery orangey-red budgie to hop into. A budgie didn't belong in my urban backyard. There are no wild budgies indigenous to the streets of Toronto. No migrating feral flocks of *Melopsittacus undulatus* in my city. In London, England, ten thousand ring-necked parakeets have roosted in their parks and green spaces for decades. One urban legend says the first few escaped from the set of *The African Queen*. But Toronto isn't that exciting. Someone loved and lost this bird. She was someone's pet. The bird didn't know enough to not be afraid of me, so I clutched her fragile body in the palm of my hand. She was instantly named Rosie and became an adored member of our family.

Love is an action. I brought the bird inside. Cleaned and inspected its body. I gave it water and a safe place to sleep. I Googled "budgies." I posted virtual missing budgie flyers on local lost pet groups on social media. I called my vet who recommended a bird specialist, but they wouldn't be open until the morning.

Love is responsible. Time will not wait for love. We had a deadline. So, I loaded my brood into the car. They chatted the whole drive asking, "Can we keep Rosie if she lives?"

Love is complicated. I lied. Rather, I prattled on making false promises that Rosie will one hundred percent be okay. I did this so the kids could pack their worries away for a couple of hours and enjoy the whole experience of the movie. Lying is sometimes loving, I rationalized.

Love is work. I did not watch the movie. Instead, I settled them into the back of the truck, laying out blankets and primping and fluffing pillows until it resembled the inside of a genie's bottle. I shuttled the children from the car to the bathroom.

I refereed fights. I cleaned the spills. I got more popcorn when the first popcorn was dropped all over the gravel. When the film ended, I found out that my cell had died, so I used my homing instincts to try to find our street without a map. It took an extra half hour, because I missed the highway entrance and made a wrong turn, but we made it.

Love is sacrifice. When we got home, I was tired and spent. I wanted to curl into my bed but instead I fed our pets. I made up the pull-out couch for the girls for a special treat. I brought them more snacks.

Love is exhilarating. I checked on the bird. She was alive! We all slept for a few hours.

Love is unfair. In the morning the girls were up before me. Their alarming cries rang out through the house. I wanted to put the pillow over my face, but I instead rolled out of bed and flew down the stairs. Rosie's tiny, feathered body was rock hard. She was on her back with her little talons in the air. On further examination, I could see a piercing. A microscopic claw wound under her wing, so small that there was almost no blood. Our cat had been mere moments away from bringing us an offering of her own affection yesterday.

Love hurts. My children were despondent. This love had been a whirlwind for them. As a mother, I tried not to curl up into a ball of regret and my own insufficiency. I brought this pain into our house. I had done nothing but prolong the inevitable. I always knew this could be the outcome, likely would be the outcome. I welcomed death and put it in their path.

Love is a memory. So, I found the children an empty shoebox and I pulled out some craft paper. The kids drew pictures on the brown paper of a bright red bird around which they wrote her name in large bubble letters of burnt sienna. They began preparing the inside of her homemade coffin, making it decorative and comfortable. A little dollhouse project for them. Tiny blankets, a pillow for her head, soft tissue paper lining. The tears turned into creative excitement.

Love is a flight of fancy. Easily shown. Easily lost. Easily replaced.

Love is digging the grave. I pressed the shovel into the compacted dirt under the winterberry tree in the backyard, while inside, the girls dried and pressed fallen flower petals between pages of their favourite books.

The night before my birthday, my mother had taken a turn for the worse. The family was called in, I met with her doctor, the paramedics stayed with us. She was sleeping. Her breathing was getting slower and more shallow. In the dim light of the kitchen, around midnight, the doctor told me it was likely to happen sometime within the night. She told me what to do afterwards. Who to call, what would happen. She was so kind.

The following morning, Mom passed away as gently and peacefully as she had lived. And I realized that was her lesson. The only lesson. Kindness. Kindness was my mom's dream — to raise and teach children who would show kindness and compassion to our most vulnerable at all times. She may have been vanishing, but her spirit remained solid.

And I think to myself now, perhaps this is the job of all mothers — to vanish. It's the ultimate, bittersweet, and beautiful kindness that we can offer. To slowly remove yourself task-by-task from your children's lives as they take them on themselves, and then to gently fade backwards into the darkness and let your progeny step into the spotlight.

Minutes after she passed away, a bright red bird flew onto the branch of the apple tree next to our little stream. Someone said that a red bird is a messenger from the spirit world, reminding you to love yourself exactly as you are. After we said some prayers and had a cry and said some kind words, my mother's PSWs and I washed and dressed her body to prepare her for the funeral home. I grasped my mother's hand and tried to burn the memory of the feeling of her thumb on my hand, her thin pale skin with the strong blue veins, and longed to feel her moving it side to side along my hand the way she always had. Her grip on my hand firm, not letting go.

I don't know where she went. I know of course that she isn't a bird, but I'll never know if she went up to some ineffable, heaven-like dimension, or stayed as she is, simply down into the earth, or perhaps particles of her went back up to the stars, where we started this whole series of essays, and where we all came from. Carl Sagan said, "The cosmos is within us. We are made of star-stuff. We are a way for the universe to know itself." Maybe the point isn't to find meaning in and amongst the two trillion or so galaxies out there, or even in the 400 billion stars in our own galaxy. Maybe the point of being here is to find meaning in our relationships with each other, in the dull day-to-day work we do here in our own homes and backyards. I don't mind trying to understand the universe though, because since we are made up of the universe, to understand it is to try and understand ourselves. When we understand ourselves, we are better able to care for each other, which we all need in our time together on this one fragile planet, in a vast and often unforgiving universe. Our relationships are not dissimilar to what Brian Cox, the British

Cosmologist said about the universe, "You dig deeper and it gets more and more complicated, and you get confused, and it's tricky and it's hard, but it's beautiful."

ACKNOWLEDGEMENTS

EMERGING: coming out, *coming into view or taking shape, or surviving and coming out from a difficult situation.*

Participating in art professionally is an enormous privilege that I do not take for granted. To write a book you need time alone. You need life experiences to draw from. You need some education in your medium. You need opportunities to share your work. And perhaps most importantly, you need a community of people around you to lift you up. For me, things started coming together almost thirty-five years after I first started writing, and I found community across the globe.

I wrote my haunted house essay *The Ghost Was the Least of our Problems* and submitted it to the *Modern Love* column and then promptly put it out of my mind. The chances of being chosen were less than one percent at the time. But then, six months later, I received the most wonderful message from Dan

Jones, the editor. I was going to be published, and on Halloween. I picked up my copy on a Sunday morning and read it over a glass of champagne knowing my life had changed, because I had changed. So, my first Thank You has to be to Dan Jones. I am eternally grateful for the remarkable care he took in editing my piece, and sharing the sage advice that he developed in the decades he has spent fostering this space for emerging writers.

Shortly afterwards, I was signed by my agent Carolyn Forde at Transatlantic who is an absolute champion of her clients and so generous with her advice and guidance. And she introduced me to my gem of an editor Pia Singhal, the talented team at ECW Press, and phenomenal copy editor Rachel Ironstone. Pia has been a joy to partner with and elevated this work to something I'm very proud of.

The *New York Times* essay was optioned by Amazon Prime for the television series *Modern Love Amsterdam*, and expertly adapted into something entirely unique by writer Maud Wiemeijer and director Mijke de Jong into the season one episode "De Geese Uit De Fles." I am so grateful to Maud for finding inspiration in my essay.

Thank you to my artist friends and mentors who spent time teaching me and supporting me, both formally and informally, in the last few years, or who stopped and took time out of your day/life/holiday to share some advice: Katherena Vermette, Andrea Bennett, Laurie Petrou, Marnie Woodrow, Rachel Matlow, Marsha Shandur, Anne Bokma, Margo MacDonald, Tracey Erin Smith, Kate Johnston, Kate Rigg, Carole Pope, Robert McQueen, Maggie Casella, Akiva Romer Segal, Michael Petrou, John Zilcosky, Kevin McGran, Elizabeth Ruth, and Ivan Coyote.

To my coven of lifelong best friends Suzanne Cheriton (the first person to suggest I submit my writing for publication), Jane Minty (thank you for your continued support in this upcoming year), Sherri Kovacs and my friend and sister-in-law Karen McOuat, Jean LaMantia, Eve Schifman, and Rebecca Wittman. And especially to Marisa Gatto, whose love and friendship (and editing talent) is a blessing.

And to my family most of all, who are also my employers and colleagues. We work together, play together, and help each other. Not a lot of people can say they have friends for siblings, I am so glad I can. Thank you especially to Geoff and Craig for reading my essays and providing feedback and Craig for his incredible historical work on our family genealogy. Thank you to my enormous extended family for sharing your versions of some of our family stories with me, especially Aunt Danielle and Uncle George and the cousins and nieces and nephews. And Miles Cruise for helping to edit my bibliography. Thank you, universe, for delivering me into the hands of these parents, who gave me access to classic literature in my home, and who encouraged my creativity and personality. Especially my Mom, who brought everyone snacks and a jug of McDonald's orange drink to every play rehearsal and dance recital.

Thank you to Tatum Holland and Georgia Grace for being wonderful and curious and patient with me through this all. The words I have in my brain to explain how much I love you could fill volumes of books.

Thank you to the writers and artists who created the films and television shows and music and books and all of the media that influenced my generation. Please see the Watch List for more information. Now more than ever, we know how essential human creativity is to our collective souls. The one thing the machines can't take from us is our own true stories in our words.

To anyone reading, thank you for being a part of the community that helps writers and especially emerging artists. Since this is my first book, I am playfully referring to myself as "emerging". I am "emerging from the shower" I will yell to my children. "I am emerging from my house to come and see you" I tell my sister over the phone, because humour is joy and I feel joyful that I accomplished this. Humour is also protective, and I am admittedly nervous with putting out my first book. And also, I think partially because by saying it out loud, repeating it to myself, maybe I'll start to believe this is all really happening.

BIBLIOGRAPHY

Aesop. (1985). The boy who cried wolf. In M. Hague (Ed.), *Aesop's Fables*. Henry Holt.

Bolin, A. (2018, August 1). The ethical dilemma of highbrow true crime. *Vulture*. https://www.vulture.com/2018/08/true-crime-ethics.html

Bowie, D. (1988). David bowie answers the Proust questionnaire. *Vanity Fair*. https://www.vanityfair.com/hollywood/2016/01/david-bowie-proust-questionnaire

Brothers Grimm. (1981). *Hansel and Gretel*. Julia MacRae Books.

Burke, E. (1757). *A philosophical enquiry into the origin of our ideas of the sublime and beautiful*. P.F. Collier & Son Company.

Bush, K. (1980). Breathing. On *Never for ever*. EMI.

Carroll, L. (2015). *Alice's adventures in wonderland: 150th anniversary edition* (T. Banchoff & M. Burstein, Eds.). Princeton University Press.

Carter, J. & Hougaard, R. (2022). *Compassionate leadership: How to do hard things in a human way.* Harvard Business Review Press.

Clover, C. J. (2015). *Men women and chainsaws.* Princeton University Press.

Colfer, E. (2009). *And another thing...* Penguin Books.

Coover, R. (1973). The babysitter. *Pricksongs & descants.* Pan Books.

Cox, B. (Writer), & Cooter, S., Holt, C., & Lachmann, M. (Directors) (2011). *Wonders of the universe.* BBC; Discovery Channel; Science Channel.

Davis, B. (2017). *The lonely life.* Hachette Books. (Original work published 1962)

Eisenberg, A., Hathaway, S., & Murkoff, H. E. (1991), *What to expect when you're expecting.* Workman Publishing Company. (Original work published 1984)

Elsesser, K. M., Lever, J. (2011). Does gender bias against female leaders persist? Quantitative and qualitative data from a large-scale survey. *Human relations, 64*(12), 1555–1578. https://doi.org/10.1177/0018726711424323

Farrell, H. (1960). *What ever happened to baby jane.* Rinehart & Company.

Fassler, J. & Manchado, C. M. (2017, October 2). How surrealism enriches storytelling about women. *The Atlantic.* https://www.theatlantic.com/entertainment/archive/2017/10/how-surrealism-enriches-storytelling-about-women/542496/

Fessler, D. M. T., & Navarrete, C. D. (2005). *The effect of age on death disgust: Challenges to terror management perspectives* for *evolutionary psychology, 3,* 279–296. https://doi.org/10.1177/147470490500300120

Frontmatter. (2004). In S. Schneider (Ed.), *Horror film and psychoanalysis: Freud's worst nightmare* (pp. i–viii). Cambridge University Press.

Heard, A. (2018, December 18). I spoke up against sexual violence — and faced our culture's wrath. That has to change. *The Washington Post*. https://www.washingtonpost.com/opinions/ive-seen-how-institutions-protect-men-accused-of-abuse-heres-what-we-can-do/2018/12/18/71fd876a-02ed-11e9-b5df-5d3874f1ac36_story.html

Hendrix, G. (2021). *The final girl support group*. Berkley.

Igou, E. R., Kinsella, E. L., & Ritchie, T. D. (2015). Zeroing in on heroes: A prototype analysis of hero features. *Journal of Personality and Social Psychology*. https://doi.org/10.1037/a0038463

Issa, N. (2023, January 14). In 2022, we watched real suffering and called it entertainment. *Deseret News*. https://www.deseret.com/2023/1/14/23528377/blonde-and-dahmer-exploiting-victims

Jackson, S. (1984). *The haunting of hill house*. Penguin. (Original work published 1959)

King, S. (1977). *The shining*. Doubleday Press.

King, S. (1979). *The dead zone*. Viking Press.

King, S. (1981). *Danse macabre*. Everest House.

King, S. (1987). *Misery*. Viking Press.

King, S. (1996). *The green mile*. Signet Books.

King, T. (2003). *The truth about stories*. House of Anansi Press.

Kundera, M. (1984). *The unbearable lightness of being*. Harper Row.

Kusby, A. (2020). *Little witches book of spells*. Chronicle Books.

Lapine, J., & Sondheim, S. (1989). *Into the Woods*. Theatre Communications Group.

Lasher, M. (2016, May 10). These stark photos provide a window into the harsh reality of victim blaming in sexual assault. *TIME Magazine.* https://time.com/4323149/sexual-assault-victim-blaming-photos/

Levin, I. (1967). *Rosemary's baby.* Random House.

Loftus, J. (2020–2021). *The Lolita Podcast.* iHeartPodcasts Network.

Michael, G. (1990) Freedom! '90. On *Listen without prejudice vol. 1.* Columbia Records.

Moriarty, L. (2018). *Nine perfect strangers.* Macmillan Australia.

Neruda, P. (1972). The dead woman. (Walsh, D. D., Trans.) *The captain's verses.* New Directions. (Original work published 1952)

Nesseth, N. (2022). *Nightmare fuel: The science of horror films.* Tor Nightfire.

Oliver, M. (1990). The summer day. *House of light.* Beacon Press.

Pinero, A. W. (1893). *Sweet lavender,* W. H. Baker & Company.

Radcliffe, A. (1826, January 1). On the Supernatural in Poetry. *The New Monthly Magazine.*

Randall, F. E. (1976). *The Watcher in the Woods.* Atheneum Books.

Sagan, Carl. (1980). *Cosmos: An appreciation.* [Manuscript/Mixed Material]. Retrieved from the Library of Congress. https://www.loc.gov/item/cosmos000052/

Sartre, J. (2007). (Macomber, C., Trans.) *Existentialism is a humanism.* Yale University Press. (Original work published 1946)

Schopenhauer, A. (1819). *The world as will and representation.*

Shakespeare, W. (1993). *Romeo and Juliet.* Dover Publications. (Original work published 1597)

Smith, V. (2024). *Hags: The demonisation of middle-aged women.* Fleet.

Sparks, N. (1996). *The Notebook.* Warner Books.

Stetson, C. P. (1892). The yellow wallpaper. A story. *The New England Magazine.*

Tuerkheimer, D. (2021, October 5). How U.S. sexual-harassment law encourages a culture of victim blaming. *TIME Magazine.*

Updike, J. (1984). *The Witches of Eastwick.* Knopf.

Van der Kolk, B. (2014). *The body keeps the score: Brain, mind, and body in the healing of trauma.* Viking.

Walker, A. (1982). *The Colour Purple.* Harcourt Brace Jovanovich.

Wallace, D. (1998). *Big fish: a novel of mythic proportions.* Pandher Books.

Winfrey, O. (2014). Age brilliantly. *O Magazine.*

Young, M. (2021, December 27). How disgust explains everything. *The New York Times.*

NO FORMAL CITATION AVAILABLE:

"Never let the truth get in the way of a good story" is often attributed to Mark Twain, 1835-1910. But that is not proven.

THE WATCH LIST

101 Dalmatians (1961, Clyde Geronimi, Hamilton Luske, &
   Wolfgang Reitherman)
9 ½ weeks (1986, Adrian Lyne)
Across The Universe (2007, Julie Taymor)
American Horror Story: Coven (2013, Ryan Murphy)
Alien (1979, Ridley Scott)
Aliens (1986, James Cameron)
Alien³ (1992, David Fincher)
All the Boys Love Mandy Lane (2006, Jonathan Levine)
Anne of Green Gables (1985, Kevin Sullivan)
Basic Instinct (1992, Paul Verhoeven)
Beetlejuice (1988, Tim Burton)
Big Fish (2003, Tim Burton)
Bon Cop/Bad Cop (2006, Érik Canuel)
Bound (1996, The Wachowskis)

Boys on the Side (1995, Herbert Ross)

Bram Stoker's Dracula (1992, Francis Ford Coppola)

Carrie (1976, Brian De Palma)

Cujo (1983, Lewis Teague)

Dirty Dancing (1987, Emile Ardolino)

Election (1999, Alexander Payne)

Feud (2017, Ryan Murphy)

Field of Dreams (1989, Phil Alden Robinson)

Friday the 13th (1980, Sean S. Cunningham)

Frozen (2013, Chris Buck & Jennifer Lee)

Ghost (1990, Jerry Zucker)

Ghostwatch (1992, Stephen Volk)

Ghostbusters (1984, Ivan Reitman)

Gilligan's Island (1964–67, Sherwood Schwartz)

Grease (1978, Randall Kleiser)

Grey Gardens (1975, Albert & David Maysles)

Halloween (1978, John Carpenter)

Haunted Honeymoon (1986, Gene Wilder)

Heathers (1988, Michael Lehmann)

Heavenly Creatures (1994, Peter Jackson)

Henry & June (1990, Philip Kaufman)

High Spirits (1988, Neil Jordan)

Hostel (2005, Eli Roth)

House Hunters (1999–present)

Hush Hush Sweet Charlotte (1964, Robert Aldrich)

I Spit on Your Grave (1978, Meir Zarchi)

Invasion of the Body Snatchers (1978, Philip Kaufman)

Law and Order (1990–2010, Dick Wolf)

Legend (1985, Ridley Scott)

Live and Let Die (1973, Guy Hamilton)

Looking for Mr. Goodbar (1977, Richard Brooks)

Misery (1990, Rob Reiner)

Mommie Dearest (1981, Frank Perry)

Mulholland Drive (2001, David Lynch)

Nine Perfect Strangers (2021, David E. Kelley)

Poison Ivy (1992, Katt Shea)

Poltergeist (1982, Stephen Spielberg)

Practical Magic (1998, Griffin Dunne)

Psycho (1960, Alfred Hitchcock)

Real World (1992–2017, Mary-Ellis Bunim & Jonathan Murray)

Rear Window (1954, Alfred Hitchcock)

Rosemary's Baby (1968, Roman Polanski)

Saw (2004, James Wan)

Scream (1996, Wes Craven)

Sex, Lies, and Videotape (1989, Steven Soderbergh)

Single White Female (1992, Barbet Schroeder)

Soylent Green (1973, Richard Fleischer)

Star 80 (1983, Bob Fosse)

Star Trek: The Next Generation (1987–1994, Gene Roddenberry)

Strait-Jacket (1964, William Castle)

Tales from the Crypt (1972, Freddie Francis)

The Amityville Horror (1979, Stuart Rosenberg)

The Babysitter (1995, Guy Ferland)

The Blair Witch Project (1999, Daniel Myrick & Eduardo Sánchez)

The Changeling (1980, Peter Medak)

The Color Purple (1985, Stephen Spielberg)

The Cook, The Thief, His Wife & Her Lover (1989, Peter Greenaway)

The Craft (1996, Andrew Fleming)

The Craft: Legacy (2020, Zoe Lister-Jones)

The Dead Zone (1983, David Cronenberg)

The Entity (1982, Sidney J. Furie)

The Exorcist (1973, William Friedkin)

The Graduate (1967, Mike Nichols)

The Green Mile (1999, Frank Darabont)

The Notebook (2004, Nick Cassavetes)

The Seven Year Itch (1955, Billy Wilder)

The Shining (1980, Stanley Kubrick)

The Sixth Sense (1999, M. Night Shyamalan)

The Terminator (1984, James Cameron)

The Texas Chainsaw Massacre (1974, Tobe Hooper)

The Town that Dreaded Sundown (1976, Charles B. Pierce)

The Unbearable Lightness of Being (1988, Philip Kaufman)

The Watcher in the Woods (1980, John Hough)

The Witches of Eastwick (1987, George Miller)

To Wong Foo, Thanks for Everything! Julie Newmar (1995,
    Beeban Kidron)

Truly, Madly, Deeply (1990, Anthony Minghella)

Urban Legend (1998, Jamie Blanks)

Warm Bodies (2013, Jonathan Levine)

What Ever Happened to Baby Jane? (1962, Robert Aldrich)

When a Stranger Calls (1979, Fred Walton)

When a Stranger Calls Back (1993, Fred Walton)

Wild Things (1998, John McNaughton)

ABOUT THE AUTHOR

ALLYSON MCOUAT is a writer with essays in publications such as the *New York Times*, the *Globe and Mail*, *Broadview* magazine and *Plenitude Magazine*. Her essay "The Ghost Was the Least of Our Problems" was optioned by Amazon Prime for season one of the *Modern Love Amsterdam* television series. By day, Allyson is an advertising copywriter and social media manager for McOuat Partnership. She often volunteers her time writing grants to support writers, artists, and cultural organizations. Allyson lives in Toronto with her two sensational daughters, Tatum and Georgia. This is her debut book.